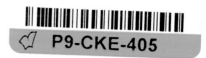

LITERATURE & THOUGHT

AND JUSTICE FOR ALL

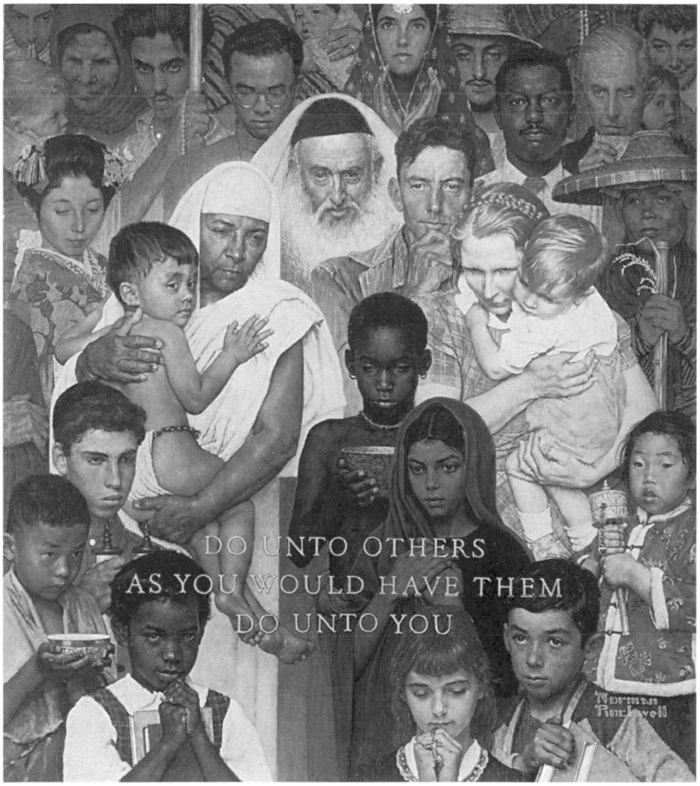
DO UNTO OTHERS
AS YOU WOULD HAVE THEM
DO UNTO YOU
Norman Rockwell

Perfection Learning

Editorial Director Julie A. Schumacher
Senior Editor Terry Ofner
Editor Linda Mazunik
Permissions Laura Pieper
Reviewers Larry Bargenquast
Ann Tharnish

Design and Photo Research
Jan Michalson
Lisa Lorimor

Cover Art THE GOLDEN RULE (detail) 1961 Norman Rockwell
Printed by permission of the Norman Rockwell Family Trust
Copyright © 2000 the Norman Rockwell Family Trust
Photo Courtesy of The Norman Rockwell Museum at Stockbridge

Acknowledgments

From *America's Dumbest Criminals* by Daniel R. Butler, Leland Gregory, and Alan Ray. Copyright © 1995 by The Entheos Group. Reprinted by permission of Rutledge Hill Press, Nashville, Tennessee.

"And Justice for All" by Johnny D. Boggs. First appeared in *Boy's Life*, October 1997 issue. By permission of Johnny D. Boggs and *Boy's Life*, published by the Boy Scouts of America.

The Bishop's Candlesticks, from *Les Misérables*, by Victor Hugo, is adapted by Lewy Olfson and reprinted from *Classics Adapted for Acting and Reading*, by Lewy Olfson (Plays, Inc., Publishers), with permission from the publisher. Copyright © 1970 by Lewy Olfson. This play is for reading purposes only; for permission to produce, write to Plays, Inc., 120 Boylston St., Boston, MA 02116.

"Could A Woman Do That?" from *Guilty or Innocent?* by Anita Gustafson (Holt, Rinehart & Winston, 1985). Copyright © 1985 by Anita Larsen. Reprinted by arrangement with Writer's House, Inc., as agent for the proprietor.

CONTINUED ON PAGE 144

1000 North Second Avenue
P.O. Box 500, Logan, Iowa 51546-0500
Tel: 1-800-831-4190 • Fax: 1-712-644-2392

Printed in the United States of America

Paperback ISBN: 0-7891-5228-2

Cover Craft® ISBN: 0-7807-9665-9

What is justice?

The question above is the *essential question* that you will consider as you read this book. The literature, activities, and organization of the book will lead you to think critically about this question and to develop a deeper understanding of justice.

To help you shape your answer to the broad essential question, you will read and respond to four sections, or clusters. Each cluster addresses a specific question and thinking skill.

CLUSTER ONE What's fair—what's not? **EVALUATE**

CLUSTER TWO Who judges? **ANALYZE**

CLUSTER THREE Punishment or mercy? **COMPARE/CONTRAST**

CLUSTER FOUR Thinking on your own **SYNTHESIZE**

Notice that the final cluster asks you to think independently about your answer to the essential question—*What is justice?*

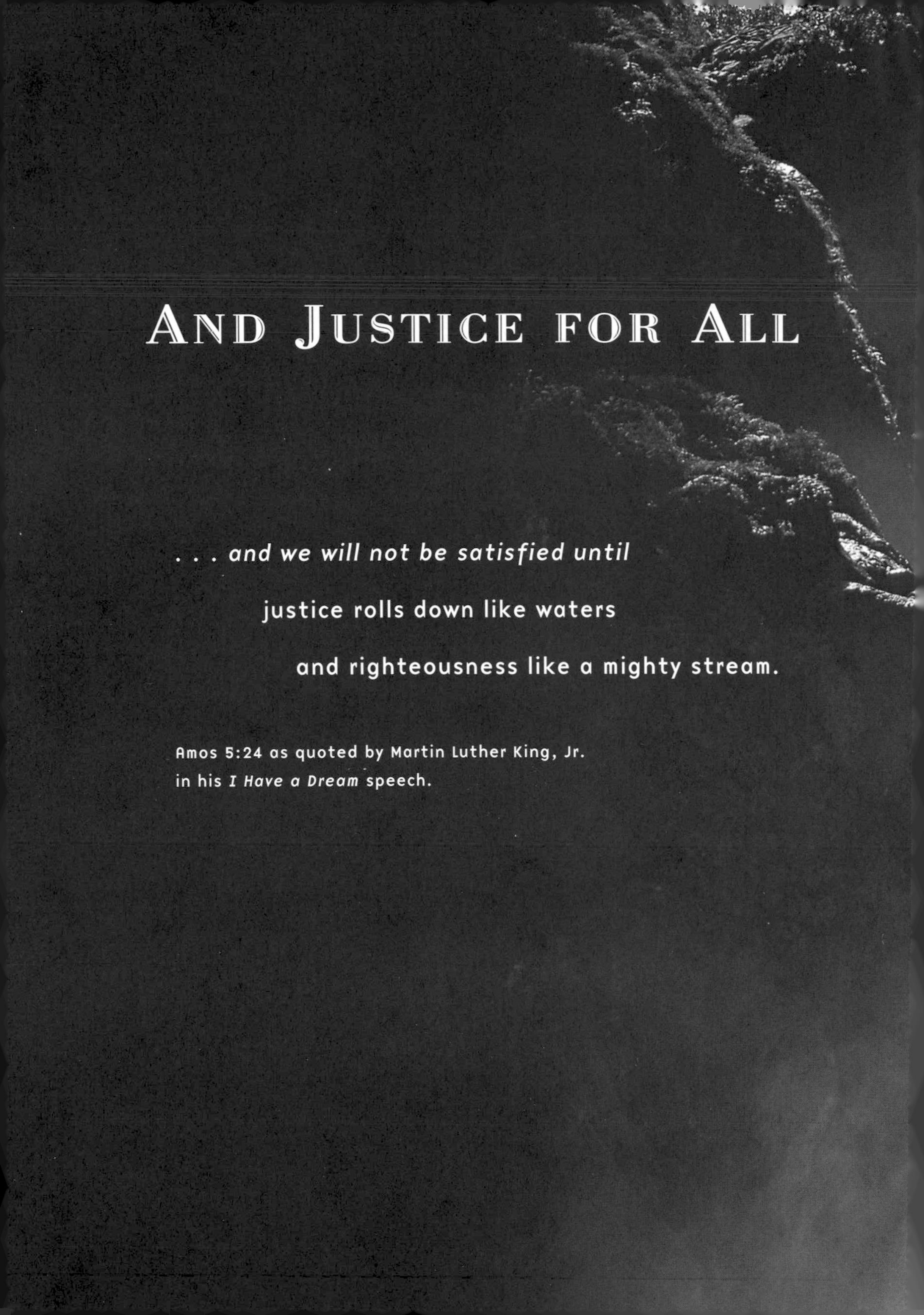

And Justice for All

. . . and we will not be satisfied until

justice rolls down like waters

and righteousness like a mighty stream.

Amos 5:24 as quoted by Martin Luther King, Jr.
in his *I Have a Dream* speech.

Table of Contents

THE QUESTION OF FAIRNESS

What if your town enforced a curfew of 10:30 p.m. because a few kids caused trouble?

What if trained dogs were regularly brought in to your school to hunt for drugs concealed in lockers?

What if you were not allowed to carry a backpack to school because one or two students were caught with concealed weapons in their packs?

These are questions of fairness and justice. Depending upon whom you ask, you will get different answers. Some might say that such laws and actions are necessary to maintain the safety of the majority. Others may point out that such practices are unfair because they assume that all young people are guilty until proven innocent. Both sides have valid arguments. It may take time—or a court ruling—before society decides which side is right.

The way in which people solve issues of fairness helps define the society in which they live. For example, in many early civilizations, justice was swift and inflexible. Often, the punishment matched the crime, as in this familiar guidance from the book of Deuteronomy in the Jewish Torah. ". . . but life shall go for life, eye for eye, tooth for tooth, hand for hand, foot for foot."

In Medieval Europe, justice was sometimes sought through *trial by combat* in which "might proved right." The knight who survived a fight to the death with an adversary proved that his cause was righteous. A similar spirit of justice later inspired the *duel* in which individuals shot at each other with pistols from a set distance. American patriot Alexander Hamilton died in such a "trial of honor" with Aaron Burr.

The historical record shows the unfortunate tendency for fairness to give way to hysterics and corruption. For example, witch trials—originating in Europe during the 1100s and lasting as late as the Salem witch trials of the late 1600s—gave rise to *trial by ordeal.* In the *ordeal by water*, a suspect's arms and legs were tied and the suspect was lowered into a pool of water. The "innocent" sank while the "guilty" floated. In the *ordeal by fire*, the suspect was forced to walk blindfolded across hot coals. If after three days there were open sores, the defendant was guilty; if the wounds were healed over, the defendant was innocent. Of course, an "innocent" declaration could be arranged. For a fee the coals would be cool enough to insure a verdict of innocent.

The point is, the establishment of fair laws is not always an easy process. In the United States, where the writing and rewriting of laws is built into the political process, agreement has been anything but smooth. Women questioned laws and social customs for decades before they won the right to vote in 1920. Native Americans did not gain voting rights in all states until 1948. And African Americans have struggled for centuries, first to gain freedom from slavery, then to gain access to fair trials, the voting booth, and economic opportunities. Indeed, the country suffered a searing civil war in the clash of differing views on the question of slavery.

So what is fairness? The answer changes, depending upon the circumstances and the people involved. One thing is certain, however. The questions of fairness will continue. Our answers will help decide who we are and how our era will be remembered.

JUSTICE THROUGH THE AGES

Egyptian Law

(ca. 4000 to 500 B.C.)

Egyptians believed their king to be a god and absolute ruler. His appointed officials served as judges and recorded legal decisions.

Babylonian Law

(ca. 2000 to 1600 B.C.)

One of the first law codes in history, the **Code of Hammurabi** contained almost 300 highly punitive laws on topics ranging from false accusations to punishments for crimes.

Hebraic (Mosaic) Law

(ca. 1700 to 600 B.C.)

The laws of Moses were written into the **Torah,** the sacred book of Judaism; commentary on the law was collected into the **Talmud.**

Greek Law

(ca. 700 to 200 B.C.)

The lawgiver Draco authored the **Draconian Code,** a series of laws with severe punishments. Solon reformed this harsh code with a new constitution that gave freemen the right to participate in assemblies, thus laying the foundation for democracy.

Roman Law

(ca. 500 B.C. to 700 A.D.)

To guide legislation, Justinian I, ruler of the eastern Roman Empire, codified and clarified existing Roman law. The result was the **Justinian Code,** upon which many countries have since based their codes of law.

American Law

(18th century to present)

American law is founded upon the **U. S. Constitution,** which empowers federal government and describes basic laws, and the **Bill of Rights,** which lays out fundamental rights of individuals. American law continues to be written by the U.S. Congress and to be interpreted by the U.S. Supreme Court.

English Common Law

(11th century to present)

Common law, based on customs and previous court rulings, developed the **trial by jury** system. The **Magna Carta** of 1215 is one of the foundations of modern justice.

Islamic Law

(ca. 600 A.D. to present)

Islamic law provides guidance in all aspects of personal and community life through the **Koran** (recorded words of the prophet Muhammad) and the **Hadith** (traditional stories).

Germanic Law

(ca. 500 A.D. to 900 A.D.)

During the Middle Ages, European kings developed their own codes of law. The methods of **trial by combat** and **trial by ordeal** were sometimes used to decide legal issues.

Canon (Church) Law

(4th century A.D. to present)

A **canon** is a collection of laws regulating a church and its clergy. By far the most extensive is that of the Roman Catholic Church, which can be traced back to first-century papal decrees.

Concept Vocabulary

You will find the following terms and definitions useful as you read and discuss the selections in this book.

acquit to free from guilt

allegation a charge yet to be proven

civil rights the rights of a citizen, especially those involving personal freedom. (The Civil Rights Movement refers to the 1960s struggle of African Americans to win basic personal liberties in the U.S.)

civil suit a court action for the recovery of a private right or claim

conscience the internal judge of one's own actions and character

criminal trial a court action for violations of public law

defendant vs. plaintiff the accused vs. the accuser

due process the idea that laws cannot contain provisions which result in unfair treatment of any individual

exonerate to vindicate, or clear from an accusation or blame

felony vs. misdemeanor a serious vs. a minor crime

judge a public official who decides matters brought before a court

justice fair and unbiased treatment

lawyer one whose profession is to represent and advise people who need legal help

legal interpretation the way courts use and apply the law as times change

letter of the law vs. spirit of the law a strict interpretation of the details of the law vs. an attempt to follow what the law is meant to do

litigation a legal contest using the judicial process

mercy lenient or compassionate treatment

prosecute to bring legal action against someone for breaking the law

trial by combat determination of guilt or innocence through a formal contest such as a joust or duel

trial by jury formal examination of evidence by a group of citizens to determine guilt or innocence of a defendant

trial by ordeal use of torture techniques to find the "truth"

verdict decision made by a jury or judge

vigilante one who takes the law into his or her own hands

CLUSTER ONE

What's fair—what's not?

Thinking Skill EVALUATING

Someone Who Saw

David Gifaldi

When the editor of my high school newspaper assigned me a story on a local historical figure for the community section of the paper, the choice seemed obvious. Edmund Catlin's name abounds in Parkdale. Catlin Road, Catlin Middle School, The Edmund S. Catlin Memorial Scholarship Fund. Still, I wanted to run it by Grandma. At eighty-three, Grandma has lived her share of local history. So on Thursday after school, with my deadline fast approaching, I borrowed Mom's car and drove out Farmington Road, clipboard at the ready. Sitting on Grandma's porch, soaking in the rays of an Indian summer sun, I waited till our talk of family and the approaching winter had wound down, then I said, "I guess Edmund Catlin would be considered a local hero."

The weathered maple rocker stopped its squeaking. Grandma clutched the top of her cardigan as though stabbed by a draft of cold air. "That's what *most* folks believe," she snapped. "You studying on heroes?"

"I'm looking for a local one," I answered. "For a story I'm writing."

She nodded, then started rocking again, her eyes fixed on the slouching barn across the road. I could tell she was holding out. Anytime she says something like "that's what *most* folks believe," you can be sure there's a story itching to bubble over.

"What do *you* believe?" I asked.

"I don't *believe* nothin'," she said. "I *know*. I seen things."

"I'm interested," I said.

"You won't like what you hear."

"I'm still interested."

Her sigh was long and deep. So deep she had to reach for her next breath, the wrinkles suddenly tightening around her eyes as if she were straining to see far beyond the barn and its stand of poplars. "What I'm remembering," she began, "happened about this time of year. Winter was in the air. Most of the leaves had turned, and a good number had fallen. Your granddad and I were just youngsters then. We was neighbors—his family and mine—so the two of us grew up together.

"Ma called us that day and asked if we'd go and pick her some mushrooms. Ma knew her mushrooms, all right. She was a real expert. Everyone knows the best time to hunt wild mushrooms is after a rain. But Ma knew which particular rain was the right one. I'd say: 'Good hard rain last night, Ma. I expect the chanterelles[1] have sprung through.' 'Not yet,' she'd say. 'Not time yet.'

"And sure enough, though I'd run out and tear the woods upside down to prove her wrong, I wouldn't find a one until Ma said *Now*. Then I'd come back with a sackful in an hour's time, and Ma would put on a big kettle for soup and Pa would make an omelette like you never saw—so thick with 'shrooms they'd be hanging out the sides.

"Well, on that particular day your granddad and I headed for our favorite hunting grounds. We picked half a sack, most of which were on the old side, but still satisfactory considering winter was breathing 'round the corner. Then we noticed how far down the sun had slunk, and we started for home. We hadn't got far when your granddad says to me, 'Getting dark awful fast. Let's take the shortcut over Devil's Rock.'

"We both knew we weren't to go up there. There was a hanging tree on that rock. Ma had told us to stay away from that place more than once. She said evil resided there. Said that at night a person could hear the crying of all the poor souls that had been hanged from the oak up there. 'Course the hanging tree hadn't seen any use in quite some time. But when this part of the country was being settled, there was no law to speak of, and people would decide for themselves about such matters as life and death. It was a hard system, and often as not it would be an innocent person swinging in the air over Devil's Rock and that was that.

"The thought of going up near such an unholy place set me to shivering. But it *was* getting dark sooner than expected. And the more I thought on it, the more I figured that Ma was most likely exaggeratin' some, so in the end I agreed.

1 **chanterelles:** edible yellow mushrooms

"There was just a hint of a path as I recall. Nothing like today. We were about to leave the trees behind, to climb up to where the granite takes over and rises dark and naked to the sky, when our ears twitched to the sound of voices. We slowed and approached closer, being careful to stay hidden in the brush.

"It was a strange and frightful sight that we saw. At the highest point of the dome-shaped rock stood the big lone oak, its gnarled fingers stretching eerily against the darkening sky. Three men stood beneath it. Two of the men were white and wore handkerchiefs across the lower part of their faces. The other man was colored. His face looked swollen. And sad, the saddest face I've seen to this day. He said nothing, just stood there with his eyes lowered, jaw closed tight, hands tied behind his back.

"As I knelt there barely breathing, I suddenly recalled the time Pa had come home late from a barn raisin'. Pa talked funny then, and he wobbled on his feet just like the two white men on the rock. Only the two men on the rock were using some mean language, too. Like, 'Say your prayers, nigger,' and 'We don't put up with nigger boys stealin' from white folks up here in Thornton County.' And all the time they was knocking him to the ground and forcing him to stand up again.

"The one man doing the most talking was well-dressed in a white shirt and a fancy black jacket. He was wearing expensive boots, too, made of snakeskin, with the heel of the right boot worn down, which I guessed was because of the way he limped on that leg.

"Your granddad nearly poked my appendix to burstin' when the fancy-dressed man drew a thick coil of rope from his saddlebag. The man threw the rope over the strongest limb of the tree—the one with a worn place on the bark—and set about forming a noose.

"'The hangin' tree!' your granddad says in the lowest of whispers. Our eyes met. We both knew what was to come, and we didn't want no part of it. So we hightailed it down the rock like a pair of jackrabbits who've heard buckshot whizzin' over their heads. I don't think we stopped once the whole way home. We made a promise to each other never to let slip a word of what we had seen. The way Ma was so superstitious about Devil's Rock, I knew for certain I'd get a whipping if she found out I was up there.

"Ma was pretty upset as it was. It was past dark by the time we got home, and she had been waiting for the mushrooms and had started in on worrying over us. I got a tongue-lashing to be sure. But she eased up on me some when she saw how I was trembling, my eyes brimming over with tears. She laid it to the fact that I was sensitive. 'Course I never said a word about what was really botherin' me. When I got to my room that night, I took hold of the calendar from Jamison's General Store and circled the date with my drawing pencil. Though I wasn't about to forget what I'd seen, I thought it was important to make a note of November twelfth somehow."

Grandma stopped there and called to Daisy, her orange tabby cat, who had just rounded the corner of the porch. Pouncing onto Grandma's lap, Daisy circled a couple times and plopped down. Then Grandma started making little cooing noises, petting Daisy from the ears all the way to the tail. The cat purred loudly in response, and Grandma seemed to forget I was even there. I cleared my throat to remind her, but to no avail. Finally I said, "Well?"

"Well what?" she said, peering into Daisy's ears and muttering something about mites.

"Is that the end?"

"The end of what?"

"Of the story!" I said in frustration.

"Oh, my, no," she answered. "News came two days later that the body of a colored man had been found strung to the hanging tree up on Devil's Rock. Ma made the sign of the cross over herself and warned us again never to go up there. She said now there was another soul to join the nightly chorus of those already dead by the tree. Pa said it was a dirty shame how some folks think they're above the law, and that no one has the right to take another's life. I never let out what I'd seen. Had no idea who the killers were anyway.

"Let me tell you, it was quite a burden for a young child to bear. I couldn't stop my mind from picturing the scene over and over. Kept seeing that poor man's face in my dreams and hearing the cruel way the other two were talking. For weeks afterward I'd wake up screaming, my bedclothes soaked with sweat. Ma thought I had the scarlet fever. Even called Doc Ferris to look me over. But there weren't nothing physically wrong."

"Did they ever find out who did it?" I interrupted.

"No, *they* never did. But I did. About six months later Pa took me to town with him to pick up some milled lumber for the new chicken house we was building. After we loaded up the wagon, we went to Jamison's for a cold drink. We were sitting out front when a car drove up. There weren't many cars around then, probably only a dozen in the whole town. When this smartly dressed man stepped down from the running board, I nearly choked on my sarsaparilla.[2] The man had a slight limp and was wearing the very same snakeskin boots I had seen on the rock. I knew they was the same because the right heel was worn away just like I remembered. Though he had on a different shirt, the jacket was exactly the same too, only freshly cleaned and pressed. But the topper was that Pa knew him! And the two commenced talking.

"'How do, Ed?' Pa said.

"'Just fine, Jim,' the man answered. 'What with summer on the rise, couldn't be better . . . Say, Jim, I'm to be running for the state legislature come election day. Sure appreciate your vote.'

"'You got it,' Pa said. 'Maybe you can teach them highbrows in the capital what it means to be an honest, hardworking man.'

"They talked for a while more. Mostly about how terrible taxes was

2 **sarsaparilla:** a beverage which tastes like root beer

getting and how Ed was going to help change all that and so on. I just sat there, numb as ice on the outside, my insides churning like a water-wheel. When we got home I ran and told your granddad what I'd discovered. Granddad had a hard time believing me. He said this man, Ed, was one of the town's leading citizens—a wealthy farmer, and a war hero to boot. But when I swore an oath of truthfulness, laying my right hand on his family's Bible and promisin' to be struck down stone dead by lightning if what I'd seen weren't true . . . well, then he believed."

"Grandma!" I cried. "You don't mean to say this Ed person was Edmund Catlin, the famous?"

"That's exactly what I mean to say."

"But . . . you mean he was never brought to justice?"

"Not in the usual sense," she replied. "I knew it would be impossible to prove anything in a court of law. For one thing, I never really saw the killer's face up on the rock. For another, this man was well-respected in the community, and the word of a young girl against him wouldn't be worth a plug nickel.[3] So I figured that any justice would have to come from me.

"You remember how I circled the date of the killing on the Jamison store calendar? Well, I decided that on the first anniversary of that colored man's death, Mr. Catlin would receive a little surprise. I used the old type-writer that Pa had picked up real cheap at an auction. Pa always had a way for fixin' things. He was fascinated with moving parts and would spend hours trying to figure how something worked. Anyway, I typed Mr. Catlin a short letter saying as how he was badly mistaken if he thought no one knew about the event of last November twelfth up on Devil's Rock. I signed my little note *Someone Who Saw.*

"He'd been elected to the legislature as expected just a week before, so I was fairly certain my message would make him stop and think a bit. It must have had a powerful effect, because the very next week in the classified section of the *Sentinel* was a brief ad stating that it would be appreciated if the person who sent the November twelfth letter would kindly make him- or herself known. And it was signed *Anonymous.*

"And did you?"

"Nope. I was too scared. No telling what a man like that might do to a young child. Besides, Ma always said living with a stained conscience is the hardest thing there is. Though I would have liked to see Mr. Catlin

3 **plug nickel:** a counterfeit coin

behind bars where he belonged, I figured that if there was even the tiniest scab of guilt on his forsaken soul, I'd make sure to scratch it and keep it alive. I sent a note every year on November twelfth to the Honorable Mr. Catlin, reminding him that truth has no secrets. Never missed a year. And always, I would sign the letter *Someone Who Saw.*

"When your granddad and I got married, I told him about my pen pal. He was surprised. Said he'd forgotten the whole affair. I said, yes, I'm sure Mr. Catlin would have tended to forget the whole thing too, if not for my anniversary notes.

"The man spent quite a few terms in the legislature. At one point he had thoughts of running for the U.S. Congress. I sent him a real telegram then, voicing my reservations about that. I said that it was one thing, a murderer being a representative of the people at the state level, but that it was another for a murderer to take up housekeeping in Washington, D.C. I'm not sure how much influence the telegram had, but he never did run for Congress. After the second war he retired from state office and became mayor of our town. Stayed in that position until he died."

"That's incredible," I said. "And he never found out who you were?"

"Oh, he found out all right. During his second term as mayor your granddad and I attended a reception the town was having in celebration of its centennial. The mayor was there, of course. Granddad and I were right polite to him, too, as I recall. The three of us stood around the bar, gabbing about the town's illustrious history and that sort of thing. At one point I asked Mr. Catlin if he remembered a terrible incident way back the last hanging on Devil's Rock, before some folks cut down the big oak and burned it long into the night soon after the killing."

"What was his reaction?"

"Oh, he got real ashen. His hand shook so, he nearly dropped his drink. He stammered that, yes, he thought he did dimly recall such an incident, and that it was one of the more unfortunate events of our area's history. Then he cocked back his head and threw down a whole glass of whiskey in one gulp. When I saw how a few drops of the liquor had dribbled onto his chin, I got out my handkerchief. 'Allow me,' I said as I dabbed real properlike at the drops. Then I sort of spread out the handkerchief in front of his face, holding it there just below his eyes, and wrinkled my brow like I was thinking hard about something.

"'What?' he said. 'What?'

"I laughed. 'Don't pay me no mind,' I said. 'I'm always seeing likenesses everywhere. Must be your eyes. You look like someone I saw once when

I was a child. Up on Devil's Rock. Funny how things stay with you like that.' His eyes nearly popped out with surprise and fear. He backpedaled as if confronting a ghost. '*You,*' he uttered before retreating into the crowd."

Grandma wet her lips. I could tell she was tired. I checked my notes from the biographical pamphlet I'd found in the library. "So it was Edmund Catlin who was responsible for making a park out of Devil's Rock," I said.

"His name's on the plaque," she replied. "Got his name on the town hall, too. And lots of other places. Thing is, he turned out to be pretty generous after a fashion. Anytime our church group needed donations to help the poor, they'd always send me to see Mr. Catlin because I always got results. I'd barely get the words out before he'd come across with a fistful of money or a blank check. Seemed like he couldn't stand me being there in his office for more than five minutes at a time."

She sighed. The sun was low over the pasture and the air had lost its warmth. "Guess the sun has given us its best today," she said, lifting Daisy from her lap. "Better get a start on supper."

I helped her out of the rocker and walked her inside. "I'll come on Saturday with the groceries," I told her as she stood at the sink with her back to me. "We can cook together."

She nodded, then turned abruptly, her chin trembling.

"He's no hero," she said in a voice I'd never heard before. "No hero a'tall."

I hugged her hard. "I know."

I drove for home then, but it was as if the car had a mind of its own the way it turned left at the Farmington fork. By the time I got to the road leading up to the park, there was only a thin ribbon of pink in the western sky, turning the big granite dome in the distance a purply blue.

The road was a mile-long series of switchbacks ending in a small parking area. The lot was empty, and I got out and walked the path to the summit, to where a few benches were spaced around a raised bed of drooping marigolds. A line of trees had gained a foothold on the rock's west side. Beneath them two picnic tables seemed to cling to a strip of grass. To the east, farms stretched out below like pieces to a puzzle. I stepped to the waist-high slab of concrete in which was embedded a small plaque bearing the names of the park's architect and several town officials, ending with EDMUND S. CATLIN, MAYOR.

It was strangely quiet in the darkening light. No birdcalls. No hum of insects. Just my breathing. My thoughts turned to the tree and to those who had died where I now stood. Suddenly a gust of wind flung itself over the rock from the unprotected east. The wind held steady, tossing the hair across my face and causing the trees to moan in its wake. For a second I thought I heard voices, and I swerved, expecting to see people on the path behind me. But I was alone.

Even as I hurried down the path to the car, I made a promise. To the wind. To Grandma. To the voices. I doubted anyone my age knew about the sad history surrounding Devil's Rock County Park. I figured it was about time they found out.

A police officer with a drug-sniffing dog inspects student lockers at a New York high school.

Crossing the Line

Nell Bernstein

When 18-year-old Susan Fleischer learned she'd have to sign a "no drugs, no drinking" contract to join the varsity soccer team, she wasn't too psyched, but she went along with it because she wanted to play. When her school's administrators searched everybody's lockers, she was even less pleased. And when they made her class leave the room one day so dogs could sniff their bags for drugs, it really bugged her.

"I didn't know what was going on," says Susan, a tall, blond high school senior from Folsom, California. "I was scared. I know they want to help the students, but they can't take away our rights in the process."

What happened at Susan's school is far from unusual. Concerned about the safety of their students, school administrators across the country are taking more and more extreme measures to weed out drugs and weapons on campus. Some schools are hiring undercover cops or private security firms to help keep students in line. Others are making students take urine tests in order to play sports and participate in other activities, or be "breathalyzed"[1] to get into the prom. A few schools have even strip-searched students they suspected of hiding contraband such as guns or drugs.

Susan had a feeling her school was going too far, but she felt helpless to change things. She asked a lot of questions and spoke her mind at a community meeting but she didn't know what else she could do. Later, she heard about a guy from a nearby town who had taken his school to

1 **"breathalyzed":** checked for alcohol content in a person's breath through the use of a device called a breathalyzer

court after a backpack search he felt was unfair. Susan was impressed. She wondered if she might have the guts to resist the next time around.

"The scary part [of taking a stand]," Susan reflects, "is that you'll be alone, that you're the only one with your idea. But I think a lot of times it takes just one person, and you'll be surprised by how many people wind up following."

In fact, high school students across the country are protesting when they feel their administrators are infringing upon their rights. Most students, like Susan, let their views be known but end up doing as they're told. Others are taking it further, sometimes all the way to the Supreme Court. These aren't necessarily rebels proclaiming their right to stash pot in their backpacks or show up trashed at the prom. A lot of them are big-time overachievers—class presidents, football captains, valedictorians[2]—who don't appreciate being treated like criminals just because they're underage.

Some of these students have become local heroes, while others have found themselves the targets of hate campaigns for daring to oppose the powers that be. Some will win their battles; others won't. But what they're learning along the way is that sometimes the only way to enjoy your rights as a citizen is to fight to preserve them.

CHARLIE GUSTIN

In his hometown of Farwell, Texas (population just over 1,000), Charlie, 17, is something of a star. He is in the National Honor Society, has been ranked third in his class at Farwell High School and has won a full scholarship to the University of Texas at Austin. So how did it come to the point where people started calling him scuzzball in the local paper—and the town police chief called him a whining coward?

It all started last year when administrators announced a new policy for extracurriculars. To participate in any activity, Charlie learned, students would have to agree to random drug tests. Having recently "nailed a killer test on the Constitution" in his government class, Charlie had a strong suspicion that drug tests were unconstitutional. "And I just thought, This is my senior year, yee haw! They can't tell me what to do." So Charlie refused to be tested, and consequently got kicked out of his activities—he even lost the lead in a play. He then went to court and sued (the school district) to get back in—on the grounds that the drug test constituted an illegal search.

2 **valedictorians:** students with highest grade point averages

Charlie's case made the news in Dallas and Amarillo (the nearest big cities). But his own town didn't exactly rally behind him. The police chief wrote an open letter to Charlie in the local newspaper saying that the reason Charlie was fighting the drug tests had to be that he was a user. As evidence, the police chief revealed what Charlie calls "my one bad thing": He'd been busted the year before for drinking beer in the park.

Johnny Atckinson, the lawyer respresenting the school district, revealed additional damaging information: He claimed that Charlie had orginally agreed to take the drug test but failed to get his paperwork in on time—"and if you know anything about drug testing, that means he had a dry-out period," says Atckinson.

Charlie himself denies this and insists he was merely fighting for his rights—and those of all students. As messy as things got, Charlie says his family, his friends and especially his girlfriend, Ashley, have stood by him. And he swears he'd do the same thing again if he had to. "This is about kids who don't want to be guilty until they prove themselves innocent," he says. "That deteriorates the trust established between the teachers and administrators and the students, and turns school into a witch hunt instead of an educational environment."

With the help of the American Civil Liberties Union (ACLU), which worked on his case after he filed it, Charlie won a temporary restraining order that allowed him to continue with his extracurriculars until he graduated. Once he went away to college, he dropped the suit. Charlie says that the experience has taught him a lot. "If you come across a policy you think is not fair, stand up," he advises. "If you're wrong, they'll prove you wrong, and that'll be the end of it. But rules were made to be challenged. What would this world be if every rule proposed were instituted?"

What's the Law?

Charlie's case, like all challenges to drug testing, falls under the Fourth Amendment of the Constitution, which protects people against unreasonable searches and seizures. In the "real" world, that means the police must have probable cause—in other words, a good reason to think you're hiding something—before they can go ahead and search you or your property. (A drug test can be considered a search of your person or body.)

The Supreme Court has ruled that while the Fourth Amendment applies to public schools, it's in a more limited way than out on the street because schools need to maintain a safe and orderly environment for learning. In 1995 the Supreme Court upheld an Oregon school's right to require drug testing of student athletes even if it didn't have reason to suspect each individual athlete of using drugs. Schools like Charlie's think that means they can go ahead and test students involved in other activities as well.

LAUREN TOKER

Lauren will be the first to tell you that her town has a problem with underage drinking. The wealthy northern California enclave[3] of Piedmont boasts one convenience store, one gas station, a couple of parks—and that's about it. "Teenagers feel like there isn't much for them to do," explains Lauren, a slender 17-year-old with sandy-brown hair, "so they resort to drinking in their free time."

The problem got particularly out of hand at school dances. "People were drinking beforehand, in locker rooms and after the dances ended," Lauren recalls. "A lot of people were getting sick." (One guy vomited on the vice principal.)

But when Piedmont High started making dancegoers huff into a breathalyzer before they could walk in the door, Lauren took offense. Maybe a lot of students were drinking before or at the prom, but she wasn't. It's not that Lauren sees herself as some kind of goody-goody, but she didn't appreciate being treated like a drunk driver just because of her age. And she didn't like having her teachers—the same ones with whom she was supposed to discuss English literature the following week—engage in a high-tech version of smelling her breath.

Lauren spoke out against the breathalyzers on Youth Radio—a program based in Berkeley, California, with which she is involved. Soon everyone, from local TV stations to *The New York Times*, picked up on the story, and before long, people on and off campus were talking about the breathalyzers at Piedmont High.

That's exactly what Lauren wanted. "I think, in general, high school students aren't considered adults with civil liberties," she says. "Administrators think they can get away with a lot just because we don't know our rights. What I'm trying to do is educate people about their rights."

Initially Lauren thought the image she was generating might make the school change its mind for fear of tarnishing its reputation. It didn't happen.

3 **enclave:** an exclusive neighborhood

But that doesn't mean she thinks she's failed. "People think that just because some teenagers can't vote and don't have all the rights adults do, our opinions don't matter," she says. "What I've learned is that that is so untrue."

What's the Law?

Hard to say. No one has ever gone to court to halt the use of breathalyzers at a high school. "It's very much an open question," says ACLU attorney Ann Brick. "I think the courts can go both ways." Although breathalyzers might be deemed less invasive than, say, a urine test, Brick says the courts ought to consider the public humiliation of undergoing a breathalyzer test, and also that the device isn't really necessary to get a sense of who's drunk and who's not.

Brenda Canady

After students from Conway High School in Conway, Arkansas, visited a local beauty academy, a wallet belonging to one of the academy's students disappeared. So the high school promptly decided to search the students' bookbags. Brenda Canady, a junior, watched as the dean of women, Connie Westbrook, started bringing the female students into a bathroom, one by one. When the first girl came back out and said the dean had asked her to take off her clothes, recalls Brenda, "We said, 'No she didn't!' We just didn't believe her."

Other girls came out and reported that Westbrook had run her fingers along the inside of their bras and the waistband of their underwear. Those girls who had asked permission to call their parents said they weren't allowed to do so because the search was "required by law." The one boy on the trip did not have to take off his clothes because, an administrator had told the girls, "girls have more places to hide things."

When Brenda was called into the bathroom, Westbrook told her to take off her overalls and lift up her shirt. Then, according to Brenda, Westbrook commented on her breast size and—failing to find the stolen wallet—asked her to put her clothes back on and go outside.

"I didn't even say anything," Brenda recalls. "I just started crying. I wanted to go home and take a bath."

Administrators *did* find the stolen wallet, but it turned up in a girl's car—not in her underwear. At first, says Brenda, all she and the six other girls wanted was an apology. But when that didn't happen, they took the school to court, claiming that their Fourth Amendment rights had been violated.

While school administrators declined to be interviewed, in a press release issued a few days after the search, Conway public school's superintendent, Ray Simon, called the search reasonable and said no student had refused to be searched, seemed upset or asked to call her parents. In her own press release, Westbrook said that what had happened did not constitute a strip search and that she did not "understand the motivation of students to steal, misstate facts, contrive stories or rebel from authority."

It took a year for the case to make its way to court. On the stand, Brenda says, a lawyer asked whether she was on drugs and what she wore at the beach. But there was some consolation for these continued embarrassments: The court ruled in the girls' favor. Each student was awarded $250 in compensatory damages (money meant to repay victims for damages). The jury also awarded $10,000 in punitive damages (money meant to make a point to the school), but on appeal that decision was overturned by the judge.

"When the [original] verdict came in," Brenda recalls, "everybody was holding hands. When we went into the hallway, everyone started screaming and yelling and hugging. I couldn't even talk."

WHAT'S THE LAW?

Since the Fourth Amendment protects against unreasonable searches, what the students' lawyers had to prove was that, under the circumstances, this search was in fact unreasonable. It wasn't too hard to do. In their complaint, the students' attorneys argued that just because there was a lack of "individualized suspicion"—in other words, a definite reason to believe that a particular girl was the thief—did not mean that the administrators had the right to search all the girls. The lawsuit also claimed that, based upon what the administrators were looking for (a wallet, as opposed to say, a loaded gun), a strip search was excessive, and therefore unreasonable.

What happened to the teens in this story was not unusual, but their responses were. Sometimes schools *do* overstep the line. When that happens, it may fall to the students to help restore the delicate balance between security and freedom.

"The kids who stand up really deserve our admiration," remarks ACLU attorney Brick. "Many of them are planning to go to college, and they are going to be dependent on teachers and administrators to write their recommendations. It takes a lot of courage to say, 'This isn't right—and this is a principle worth sacrificing for.'"

Innocent Have I Been Tortured, Innocent Must I Die

Johannes Junius, with Milton Meltzer

PRISONER OF STATE

It is hard for us today to imagine what it was like to be the victim of a long-ago witchcraft trial; the records of such cases are written by the authorities, not by the victims. Yet we do at least have the record of how it felt for one innocent who went through its agonies. . . .

One of the most famous witchcraft trials in history occurred in the cathedral city of Bamberg, Germany, in 1628. The burgomaster, or mayor, of the town, Johannes Junius, was himself accused of witchcraft. The record of the trial is in the town library, which also contains a letter that Junius wrote to his daughter Veronica during the trial. The letter, which was smuggled out of prison, includes painful and moving details, and it suggests how little the official records convey the courage and suffering of witch-hunt victims.

Many hundred thousand good nights, dearly beloved daughter Veronica.

Innocent have I come into prison, innocent have I been tortured, innocent must I die. For whoever comes into the witch prison must become a witch or be tortured until he invents sometime out of his head and—God pity him—bethinks him of something. I will tell you how it has gone with me. When I was the first time put to the torture, Dr. Braun, Dr. Kötzendöfer, and two strange doctors were there. Then Dr. Braun asks me, "Kinsman, how come you here?" I answer, "Through falsehood, through misfortune." "Hear, you," he says, "you are a witch; will you confess it voluntarily? If not, we'll bring in witnesses and the executioner for you." I said, "I am no witch, I have a pure conscience in the matter; if there are a thousand witnesses, I am not anxious, but I'll gladly hear the witnesses."

Now the chancellor's son was set before me . . . and afterward Hoppfens Elsse. She had seen me dance on Haupts-moor. . . . I answered: "I have never renounced God, and will never do it—God graciously keep me from it. I'll rather bear whatever I must." And then came also—God in highest Heaven have mercy—the executioner, and put the thumb-screws on me, both hands bound together, so that the blood ran out of the nails and everywhere, so that for four weeks I could not use my hands, as you can see from the writing. . . . Thereafter they first stripped me, bound my hands behind me, and drew me up[1] in the torture. Then I thought heaven and earth were at an end: eight times did they draw me up and let me fall again, so that I suffered terrible agony. . . .

And this happened on Friday, June 30, and with God's help I had to bear the torture. . . . When at last the executioner led me back into the

1 **drew me up:** a reference to the torture technique called *drawing* in which a person's arms and legs are stretched in opposite directions

prison, he said to me: "Sir, I beg you, for God's sake confess something, whether it be true or not. Invent something for you cannot endure the torture which you will be put to; and, even if you bear it all, yet you will not escape, not even if you were an earl, but one torture will follow after another until you say you are a witch. Not before that," he said, "will they let you go, as you may see by all their trials, for one is just like another. . . ."

And so I begged, since I was in wretched plight, to be given one day for thought and a priest. The priest was refused me, but the time for thought was given.

Now, my dear child, see in what hazard I stood and still stand. I must say that I am a witch, though I am not—must now renounce God, though I have never done it before. Day and night I was deeply troubled, but at last there came to me a new idea. I would not be anxious, but, since I had been given no priest with whom I could take counsel, I would myself think of something and say it. It were surely better that I just say it with mouth and words, even though I had not really done it; and afterwards I would confess it to the priest, and let those answer for it who compel me to do it. . . . And so I made my confession, as follows; but it was all a lie.

Now, follows, dear child, what I confessed in order to escape the great anguish and bitter torture, which it was impossible for me longer to bear. . . .

Then I had to tell what people I have seen [at the witches' Sabbath]. I said that I had not recognized them. "You old rascal, I must set the executioner at you. Say—was not the Chancellor there?" So I said yes. "Who besides?" I had not recognized anybody. So he said: "Take one street after another, begin at the market, go out on one street and back on the next." I had to name several persons there, then came the long street. I knew nobody. Had to name eight persons there. Then the Zinkenwert—one person more. Then over the upper bridge to the Georthor, on both sides. Knew nobody *again. Did I know nobody in castle—whoever it might be, I should speak without fear. And thus continuously they asked me on all the streets, though I could not and would not say more. So they gave me to the executioner, told him to strip me, shave me all over, and put me to the torture. "The rascal knows one on the market-place, is with him daily, and yet won't name him." By that they meant Dietmayer: so I had to name him too.*

Then I had to tell what crimes I had committed. I said nothing. . . . "Draw the rascal up!" So I said that I was to kill my children, but I had killed a horse instead. It did not help. I had also taken a sacred wafer, and had desecrated it. When I had said this, they left me in peace.

Now, dear child, here you have all my confession, for which I must die. And they are sheer lies and make-up things, so help me God. For all this I was forced to say through fear of the torture which was threatened beyond what I had already endured. For they never leave off with the torture till one confesses something; be he never so good, he must be a witch. Nobody escapes, though he were an earl. . . .

Dear child, keep this letter secret so that people do not find it, else I shall be tortured most piteously and the jailers will be beheaded. So strictly is it forbidden. . . . Dear child, pay this man a dollar. . . . I have taken several days to write this: my hands are both lame. I am in a sad plight. . . .

Good night, for your father Johannes Junius will never see you more. July 24, 1628.

Dear child, six have confessed against me at once: the Chancellor, his son, Neudecker, Zaner, Hoffmaisters Ursel, and Hoppfens Elsse—all false, through compulsion, as they have all told me, and begged my forgiveness in God's name before they were executed. . . . They know nothing but good of me. They were forced to say it, just as I myself was. . . .

Television scenes with actor Raymond Burr

THE LAW VS. JUSTICE

DAVE BARRY

Most of us learn how the United States legal system works by watching television. We learn that if we obey the law, we will wind up chatting and laughing with attractive members of the opposite sex when the program ends, whereas if we break the law, we will fall from a great height onto rotating helicopter blades.

Some television shows explain the legal system in greater detail: they show actual dramatizations of court trials. The best such show was "Perry Mason," which starred Raymond Burr as a handsome defense attorney who eventually gained so much weight he had to sit in a wheelchair.

"Perry Mason" was set in a large city populated almost entirely by morons. For example, the prosecutor, Hamilton Burger, was so stupid that the people he prosecuted were always innocent. I mean *always.* I imagine that whenever Hamilton arrested a suspect, the suspect heaved a sigh of relief and hugged his family, knowing he would soon be off the hook.

Now you'd think that after a while Hamilton would have realized he couldn't prosecute his way out of a paper bag, and would have gone into some more suitable line of work, such as sorting laundry. But he kept at it, week after week and year after year, prosecuting innocent people. Nevertheless, everything worked out, because in this particular city the criminals turned out to be even stupider than Hamilton: they always came to the trials, and, after sitting quietly for about twenty minutes, lurched to their feet and confessed. The result was that Perry Mason got a reputation as a brilliant defense attorney, but the truth is that anyone with the intelligence of a can of creamed corn would have looked brilliant in this courtroom.

The major problem with "Perry Mason" is that it is unrealistic: Perry Mason and Hamilton Burger usually speak in understandable English words, and by the time the trial is over everybody has a pretty good grasp of the facts of the case. In real life, of course, lawyers speak mostly in Latin, and by the time they're done nobody has the vaguest idea what the facts are. To understand why this is, you have to understand the history of the U.S. legal system.

In the frontier days, our legal system was very simple: if you broke a law, armed men would chase you and beat you up or throw you in jail or hang you; in extreme cases, they would hang you, then beat you up in jail. So everybody obeyed the law, which was easy to do, because basically there were only two laws:

- No assaulting people.
- No stealing.

This primitive legal system was so simple that even the public understood it. The trials were simple, too:

SHERIFF: Your honor, the defendant confessed that he shot his wife dead.

JUDGE: Did he admit it freely, or did you have your horse stand on him first, like last time?

SHERIFF: No sir. He admitted it freely.

JUDGE: Fair enough. String him up.

The trouble with this system was that it had no room for lawyers. If a lawyer had appeared in a frontier courtroom and started tossing around terms such as "habeas corpus," he would have been shot.

So lawyers, for want of anything better to do, formed legislatures, which are basically organizations that meet from time to time to invent new laws. Before long, the country had scads of laws—laws governing the watering of lawns, laws governing the spaying of dogs, laws governing the production and sale of fudge, and so on—and today nobody has the slightest idea what is legal and what is not. This has led to an enormous demand for lawyers. Lawyers don't understand the legal system any better than the rest of us do, but they are willing to talk about it in an impressive manner for large sums of money. In today's legal system, the frontier murder trial would go like this:

SHERIFF: Your honor—

DEFENSE ATTORNEY: I object. In his use of the word "your," the witness is clearly stipulating the jurisprudence of a writ of deus ex machina.

PROSECUTING ATTORNEY: On the contrary. In the case of *Merkle v. Barnbuster,* the Court clearly ruled that an ex post facto debenture does not preclude the use of the word "your" in the matter of ad hoc quod erat demonstrandum.

DEFENSE ATTORNEY: Oh yeah? Well Carthaginia delendo est.

▲ ▲ ▲

This goes on for several hours, until everybody has forgotten what the trial was about in the first place and the defendant is able to sneak out of the courtroom, unnoticed.

The Evening Standard.
NEW BEDFORD, SATURDAY, JUNE 10, 1893—TWELVE PAGES.
TWO CENTS.
THE
Great Murder Trial
IS
EVERYBODY
EXCITING AN
Full reports given through
creasing business, built
OUR
HE DEFENSE?
Convincing
owlton Broug
LIZZIE B
A Verdict o
Tumult
VINDICATED,
An Extraordinary Scene in th
Bedford Court Room
IN A FAIN
WFUL ARRAIGNME
on Promises to Off
vidence Against
Jurors Visit
he Tragedy
ZIE BOR
On the C
Murder.
e Move Made
Police,
Lizzie A. Borden

Could a Woman Do That?

Anita Gustafson

It was Thursday, August 4, 1892, and the day promised to be as hot and muggy as the day before had been.

At 6:15 A.M. Bridget Sullivan woke. Her attic room in the Borden house at 92 Second Street, Fall River, Massachusetts, was sweltering. She felt ill but she had work to do, so she dragged herself out of bed and down the narrow back stairs.

Her routine was unchanging, but by noon life would be much less ordered and much more terrifying. The events in one of the most famous murder cases in America would occur before then, events familiar to many but mystifying to all. Witnesses' testimony told what had happened that morning.

6:30 A.M.

By now Abby Borden had come downstairs to tell Bridget what to prepare for breakfast. Then she joined John Vinnicum Morse, an overnight guest, in the sitting room. Morse was the oldest brother of Andrew Borden's first wife (Abby was his second), and Andrew relied on him for financial advice. (Lizzie later testified that her father and uncle had sat up late the night before, talking about money in voices that carried and "annoyed" her.)

6:35 A.M.

Andrew came down in a white shirt, black bow tie, and vest. He always dressed in a black woolen suit for business, no matter how hot the day. He placed the key to his locked bedroom on the sitting-room mantel and went out to unlock the barn. He picked up some pears that had fallen from the trees there and brought them into the house. Before he joined his wife and Morse, he washed his face and hands at the kitchen sink. (Andrew was wealthy but his home was small, short on convenience, comfort, and privacy.)

7:00 A.M.

It was 89° already. The Borden daughters didn't eat breakfast with the others. Emma wasn't home, and Lizzie didn't come down. The Bordens felt ill, too, but they ate for an hour, heavy foods like buttered johnnycakes, freshly baked wheat bread, ginger-and-oatmeal cookies with raisins, leftover mutton,[1] leftover mutton soup, coffee with thick cream, fruit.

8:00 A.M.

With breakfast over, Abby told Bridget to wash the windows. She herself started dusting the first floor, while Andrew and Morse relaxed in the sitting room.

8:40 A.M.

Morse stood, saying he would walk to visit some family a mile and a half away. Abby reminded him of dinner; he promised to be back by noon. Andrew went with him to unlock the kitchen doors, stepping outside to talk privately with him. Bridget heard their lowered voices as she washed the dishes. Andrew called, "Come back to dinner, John," before he reentered, relocked the door, and prepared for his day as usual. He brushed his teeth at the sink, took his bedroom key from the mantel, drew a basin of water for his washstand, climbed the back stairs.

9:00 A.M.

Lizzie descended the front stairs, stopped to speak with Abby, came to the kitchen to make herself coffee. When Andrew came down, Lizzie gave him a letter to Emma and asked him to mail it. Bridget's queasy stomach revolted then, and she dashed to the backyard. When she returned, Abby was waiting in the dining room to remind her to wash the windows. Andrew had left. Lizzie was gone, probably back upstairs in her room.

9:30 A.M.

Abby went up the front stairs to tidy the room in which John Morse slept. Bridget never saw her alive again.

10:45 A.M.

Bridget had finished washing the windows in the sitting room. She still felt rotten. She decided to go to her room and lie down. The front doorbell

1 **mutton:** meat of a sheep

stopped her. She answered it, surprised to find someone had locked the door and thrown the bolt as well. That wasn't unusual at night, but this was broad daylight! "Oh, pshaw!" she said, annoyed. She heard someone laugh at the top of the stairs, and she turned. It was Lizzie.

And it was Andrew at the door, carrying a roll of papers. Lizzie came down. She mentioned that Abby had gone out in answer to a note from a sick person. Andrew was surprised. It was hot and his wife hadn't been feeling well herself. He didn't either. He took the key from the mantel, went up the back stairs to his bedroom, came down a short while later to nap in the sitting room.

Bridget decided against her nap. She took her window-washing ladder and basin into the dining room, where Lizzie was ironing handkerchiefs. Lizzie asked Bridget if she planned to go out. Bridget said she didn't know; she felt ill. Lizzie ironed as Bridget finished the windows and took her gear into the kitchen. When she returned, Lizzie told her about a sale of dress fabric. Bridget said, "I am going to have one," but the nap would come before she bought the material to make a new dress. She trudged up the back stairs to her room to lie down. She heard the City Hall bell ring. An hour until noon.

11:00 A.M.

Next door, Adelaide Churchill left her house to buy groceries. On her way home, she saw Bridget rushing home white-faced from Dr. Bowen's house across the street and wondered if someone was sick at the Bordens'.

Once inside her kitchen, she looked from her window at the Bordens' back door. Ten yards away Lizzie leaned behind the screen door, holding her head, and with an excited, upset expression. Mrs. Churchill called, "Lizzie, what is the matter?"

Lizzie turned, as if startled. "Oh, Mrs. Churchill, please come over! Someone has killed Father!"

Minutes later, Mrs. Churchill had come around the four-foot-high fence separating the two houses. She asked Lizzie where her father was and pushed open the door to the sitting room. (Later, at the trial, a prosecuting attorney would detail Andrew's ten head wounds, illustrating his words on a plaster cast of the old man's skull.) Andrew's wounds were still fresh when Mrs. Churchill saw him, but she didn't take time to count slashes. She glanced, gasped, and returned to the kitchen.

"Where were you when it happened?" she asked Lizzie.

"I was in the barn. . . . I went there to get a piece of iron."

"Where is your mother?"

Quietly, Lizzie said, "I don't know. . . . She got a note to go see someone who is sick." Then Lizzie asked for a doctor, saying Dr. Bowen wasn't home.

Mrs. Churchill ran to find her hired man and tell him to fetch another nearby physician. A news dealer overheard her. When she left he phoned the *Fall River Globe* to give them the exclusive on a "knife slashing."

11:15 A.M.

The news dealer called the police.

Dr. Bowen was already there when Mrs. Churchill got back, asking for a sheet to cover Andrew's body. Bridget knew where the linens were kept, but she was terrified to get them alone. The killer might be lurking. Mrs. Churchill went with her to Andrew's and Abby's bedroom to get a sheet. When he'd covered Andrew, Dr. Bowen left to send a telegram to Emma. Mrs. Churchill again asked Lizzie where her mother was.

"I wish someone would try to find her. I thought I heard her come in," Lizzie said.

Since Bridget was still frightened, Mrs. Churchill again went with her, this time up the front stairs. Moments later Mrs. Churchill was back, sitting at the kitchen table, her hands shaking. "She's up there," she said.

Dr. Bowen returned and learned of the discovery of Abby's body. He climbed the front stairs to the guest room. Abby lay in a pool of blood, her head nearly separated from her body. The blood from her nineteen blows was dark and congealed. She'd died before her husband.

There was no sign of struggle anywhere. Even the fringed bedspread Abby had been smoothing was still in place, unwrinkled. The killer had surprised both victims and vanished, moving unseen and unheard through the small house at 92 Second Street that had no privacy but many locked doors.

There were few clues in the case—so few that Andrew's and Abby's funeral was interrupted so police could collect their heads for the evidence contained in the slashes. And inquest testimony and other evidence was confusing.

When Bridget was questioned at the inquest, she was terrified *she* would be arrested. All she could add to what she'd already told authorities was that the Borden household was unhappy and tense. Andrew had begun locking his and Abby's bedroom because in the last year, Abby's trinkets had been stolen and their room ransacked. Andrew thought someone in the house was responsible. But Bridget had no motive to murder Andrew and Abby Borden. She said she stayed on only because Abby begged her to.

Emma had a motive. She'd resented Abby since the woman married her father thirty years ago when she was nine and Lizzie two. Her ill feeling had grown lately when Andrew gave his wife a farm, land that Emma thought should belong to her and Lizzie. Andrew gave his daughters gifts of equal value, but the gift to his wife rankled, and the thought that there might be more was alarming. Morse's financial advice might end in Andrew's making a will . . . and it might favor Abby. But Emma couldn't have committed the murders. She had an alibi: She was visiting friends in another town when they occurred.

No one checked her alibi, but they looked into John Morse's. It was watertight. The relatives he'd been visiting at the time of the murders firmly supported it.

Lizzie had no alibis other than her own statements, and unfortunately for her, her statements changed each time she made one, at, before, and after the inquest. Sometimes she said she was in the barn during the time of the murders. Once she said she went there to get material to repair a screen, other times for iron to make sinkers for her fish line, and still other times to eat pears. She also said she'd been eating pears under a tree or had been in her room mending lace during the time in question.

Her confusion at the inquest could have been caused by being forced to create an alibi on the spur of the moment. It could have been an attempt to "cover up" for someone else. (Books have been written "proving" Bridget's or Emma's guilt.) Or it could have been the effect of morphine prescribed by her doctor to ease the horror of her father's death. (They were close. When a child, she'd given him her small, gold ring as a bond; he was buried wearing it.)

Whatever the source of Lizzie's confusion, the authorities had none. They knew she'd been as upset as Emma about Andrew's gift to Abby. They knew she'd tried to buy deadly prussic acid the day before the murders, supposedly to use in cleaning a sealskin coat. (Prussic acid couldn't be used for that and the druggist hadn't sold it to Lizzie, but the attempt to buy it showed murderous intent.) They knew she'd been at home during the ninety minutes in which the murders were committed, even though she claimed not to have heard anything unusual. They'd checked the loft of the barn and found thick dust undisturbed on its floor. And they'd found several axes in the house, including one with a freshly broken handle. The axe head was covered with ashes, as if someone had tried to disguise that it had been washed.

Lizzie's defense attorney was barred from the inquest. Under

Massachusetts law a prosecutor could choose to hold an inquiry before a judge, and a suspect didn't have the right to be represented by counsel. Witnesses could be sworn and both the judge and the prosecutor had the right to question them.

At the end of the third day, August 11, Lizzie Borden was charged with the murders and arrested. The next morning a preliminary hearing was set for August 22.

In Lizzie Borden's preliminary hearing, two of the major issues that would later collide at her trial surfaced. One argued for her innocence in the murders. An expert had tested all the axes and hatchets found in the Borden basement. He had discovered no traces of blood on any of them. The gray hairs adhering to one had come from a cow. Without an easily and rapidly hidden murder weapon, the prosecution's success in convicting Lizzie would be hampered. She hadn't had either the time or the opportunity to get rid of a weapon off the premises.

The other major issue dealt in a less evidential way with the likelihood of Lizzie Borden's guilt. She was a woman, and the society of the time found it difficult to believe a woman could murder her parents. Judge Blaisdell thought a woman could. He said, "Suppose for a single moment a *man* was standing there. He was found close by the guest chamber, which to Mrs. Borden was a chamber of death. Suppose a *man* had been found in the vicinity of Mrs. Borden—was the first to find the body—and the only account he could give was the unreasonable one that he was out in the barn looking for sinkers—then he was out in the yard—then he was out for something else—would there be any questions in the minds of men what should be done with such *a man*?" He decided Lizzie was "probably guilty" and sent her to the grand jury.

The grand jury's job is to inquire and investigate behind closed doors. The grand jury decides if the accused should be ordered to stand trial (indicted). Indicted persons are then arraigned, or ordered to appear in court, to be identified, hear the charges against them, and plead guilty or not guilty. They are tried before a petit jury. (*Petit* is a French word meaning small.) The "small" jury is made up of people drawn by lot from a list of voters. It listens to evidence from witnesses, then decides whether to release (acquit) a person from being tried (the defendant) or convict him or her. When the grand jury that would decide whether Lizzie Borden should go to trial convened in November, it listened to evidence for two weeks without an indictment. But on December 1, the grand jury reconvened to hear a witness testify about a dress.

Lizzie had burned the dress she'd worn during the crucial ninety minutes because it had brown paint stains. Brown is the color of dried blood. The grand jury decided it was high time Lizzie appeared before a petit jury.

Her trial began on June 5, 1893. A panel of three Superior Court judges presided because Massachusetts law required such a panel in cases where a verdict of guilty meant death. One hundred and eight possible jurors were questioned before twelve were chosen.

The prosecution's case against Lizzie was based on her confused testimony at the inquest, the burned dress, and the broken-handled axe—the murder weapon, they said. Its cutting edge fit the Borden's wounds exactly.

Lizzie's defense managed to strike the testimony of the three inquest witnesses who knew about the prussic-acid episode. The jury couldn't use any of this information when deciding on its verdict. Emma testified she had suggested that Lizzie burn the dress. And the defense demolished the credibility of the broken-handled axe as the murder weapon.

The defense went further, producing witnesses who said they had been in the barn's loft *after* the time that Lizzie said she'd been there. If the dust on the floor wasn't disturbed, perhaps police investigators hadn't looked carefully enough. Other defense witnesses described strange people seen lurking around the Borden house. Still more witnesses testified as to Lizzie's churchgoing, Sunday-school-teacher character.

The defense noted that it didn't have the burden of proof. It didn't have to prove who *had* murdered the Bordens, only that Lizzie couldn't have. Lizzie, said the defense, was innocent. A woman couldn't do such a thing. A guilty verdict would result in her death in the electric chair. "You are trying a capital case," the defense attorney said, "a case that involves a human life, a verdict in which against her calls for the imposition of but one penalty, and that is that she shall walk to her death." The defense thus clarified the jury's hard decision—set Lizzie Borden free or execute her.

The prosecution's closing arguments hit hard on the idea that somebody in the house had to have committed the murders. It was locked inside and out, right down to the closet at the head of the stairs and the barn door. On the day of the murders, the front door was locked and bolted. Because there were no halls in the house and each room had to be entered either from the back or front stairs or from another room, it was highly improbable that a stranger could scuttle through, hide, and vanish.

Woman of good character or not, there were excellent reasons why Lizzie wanted her parents dead. A woman was physically able to kill them with an axe, and such a woman would not be stopped by "feminine" emotion. "They are no better than we," the prosecution said. "They are no worse than we. If they lack in strength and coarseness and vigor, they make up for it in cunning, in dispatch, in celerity,[2] in ferocity. If their loves are stronger and more enduring than those of men, on the other hand, their hates are more undying, more unyielding, more persistent." Contrary to what the defense claimed, a woman could do this; Lizzie was guilty beyond a reasonable doubt.

On June 20, 1893, the case went to the jury after one of the judges charged them. "You have listened with attention to the evidence in this case and to the arguments of the defendant's counsel. It now remains for me, acting in behalf of the court, to give you such aid towards a proper performance of your duty," he said.

He went on to destroy the prosecution's case. He mentioned again Lizzie's fine character, to excuse her confused statements as to her whereabouts when the murders were committed, to urge the jury to ignore what they read in the newspapers and seek only the truth. If they could do that, he said, the trial would "express in its results somewhat of that justice with which God governs the world."

With that remarkable and partisan[3] charge ringing in their ears, the jury took only an hour and six minutes to bring in a verdict.

What do you think? Was Lizzie Borden guilty? Or was she innocent of the crime and guilty only of being in the wrong place at the wrong time?

VERDICT
Lizzie Borden
Found Not Guilty

"*Not guilty*," the jury foreman said.

Lizzie sank into her chair and covered her face with her hands. Spectators in the courtroom cheered and waved their hats and handkerchiefs. People lined up to shake her hand and murmur "God bless you." They held up babies for her to kiss. They'd read the newspapers, and they shared the popular view: "A woman couldn't do such a thing."

She and Emma returned to a banker's house in Fall River. Guests poured into the house, crowds gathered outside, and shortly after 10:00

2 **celerity:** swift action
3 **partisan:** one-sided

a band arrived. People inside and out sang "Auld Lang Syne."

Even though Lizzie had testified that Andrew had left a will, none was found. She and Emma inherited a fortune. They bought a large house in the best section of town and named it Maplecroft. But not long after the "outsider" newspeople left, townspeople who had supported Lizzie during the trial ostracized her. No new suspect was found, and the townspeople began to wonder about Lizzie's innocence.

Three years after she was acquitted of murder, Lizzie shoplifted two porcelain paintings from an art gallery. The gallery owner threatened to take her to court unless she "confessed" to the murders. He said he just wanted to know the truth and promised to keep the confession secret.

Perhaps Lizzie dreaded another imprisonment. She went to a nearby typewriter and wrote: "Unfair means force my signature here admitting the act of August 4, 1892, as mine alone."

Legal experts who later studied the records of the case conclude that Lizzie's typed "confession" was the truth. They say the trial was conducted unfairly. When one of the three presiding judges instructed the jury, he said that there was no direct evidence and that a respectable woman like Lizzie couldn't have killed her parents. When Lizzie's inquest testimony and that of the three prussic-acid witnesses was barred, the jury was almost forced to acquit. Evidence was suppressed or incorrectly stated by the defense. Some Fall River residents felt some witnesses helped Lizzie simply because she was one of them.

Following a quarrel with Lizzie, Emma moved from Maplecroft, and the two never spoke again. But Emma firmly believed in her sister's innocence. Twenty years after the trial she said, "If Lizzie had done that deed, she could never have hidden the instrument of death so that the police would never find it."

The case is still unsolved.

RESPONDING TO CLUSTER ONE

WHAT'S FAIR—WHAT'S NOT?

Thinking Skill EVALUATING

1. In "Someone Who Saw," Grandma says that Edmund Catlin was never brought to justice "in the usual sense." **Evaluate,** or judge, if Grandma's way of dealing with Catlin's wrongdoing was the best method of justice or not.
2. Using a chart such as the one below, **evaluate** the school policies in each case study from "Crossing the Line." Give at least one argument supporting and opposing each school policy.

School Policy	Arguments Supporting	Arguments Opposing
restrictive sports contracts		
locker and bag searches		
use of undercover police		
drug tests to play sports		
breathalyzer		
strip searches		

3. In "The Law vs. Justice," Dave Barry uses **satire** to make a point about the American legal system. In satire, a writer makes fun of people or ideas in order to make a point. Summarize one or more of the points that Barry is making and state whether or not you agree with him.
4. If you were a juror in the murder trial of Lizzie Borden, what would your verdict be? Choose three reasons to support your verdict.

Writing Activity: Look at It My Way

Choose one judgment from the selections in Cluster One and either defend or oppose that decision. Write a speech persuading others to agree with your viewpoint.

A Strong Persuasive Speech

- clearly states a position on the issue given
- supplies at least three reasons or details to support that position
- ends with a memorable summary statement of the position held

CLUSTER TWO

WHO JUDGES?

Thinking Skill ANALYZING

And Justice for All

Johnny D. Boggs

A gavel sounds sharply in Harrison County Circuit Courtroom No. 3 in Gulfport, Mississippi. The room falls silent—court is now in session. The judge administers the oath. With right hands raised, potential jurors agree to reach a verdict according to the law and the evidence.

"You may be seated," the judge says. "The bailiff will call the first case."

This is real life about real crime and real punishment. But something is different.

Welcome to teen court—where the lawyers, jurors and the defendant are all kids.

Trial by Peers

The country's first teen court began in Odessa, Texas, in 1983. Harrison County's version held its first trial in 1995.

The idea is to educate teenagers about our legal system, giving them experience as defense attorneys, prosecutors, bailiffs and jurors.

But this isn't pretend.

Kids ages 8 to 18 are actually on trial for everything from speeding and shoplifting to assault and doing drugs. While the United States Constitution provides all citizens with the right to a trial by jury, teen court takes it one step further.

"We try to use peer pressure as a positive influence," says Don W. Fredericks, an adult who is executive director of the Harrison County Teen Court.

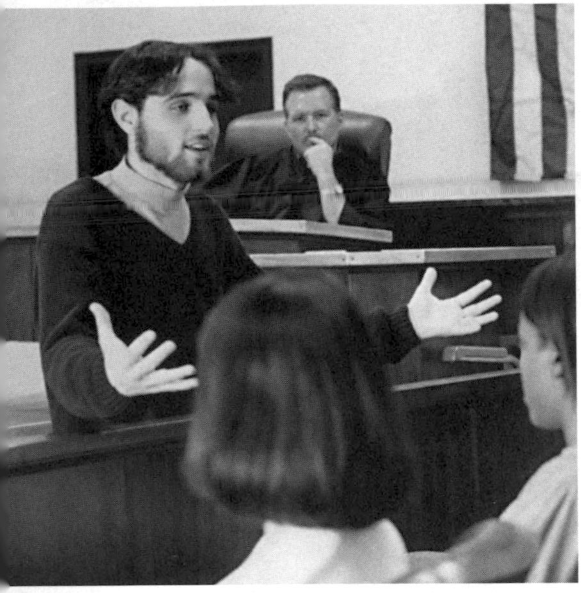

Court officials figure that teenagers who get in trouble care more about what kids their own age think than adults and will respect their peers' decisions more.

How It Works

Teen courts don't determine a defendant's guilt or innocence. The youth on trial has already pleaded guilty, agreeing to undergo a hearing in which the punishment will be decided. Students serving as defense attorneys seek an easier punishment.

"I look the jurors in the eye and say my client is sorry for what happened," says Boyd James IV, 14, who has served as a defense attorney in Harrison County's program. "I'll say he's *really* sorry and ask the jury to give a lighter sentence."

Is he convincing?

"I guess so," Boyd says. "Everybody I've represented got the lowered sentence."

The prosecutor, however, wants the maximum punishment. For a teenager guilty of shoplifting, Gulfport prosecutor Joey Robinson, 13, might ask the jury to sentence the wrongdoer to be banned from the store where he stole merchandise, write a two-page apology to the store manager and write a three-page report for the court on why shoplifting is wrong.

The Jury Deliberates

After listening to testimony, the 12 teenage jurors must discuss the case among themselves. All jurors must then agree on the punishment.

"You listen to all the evidence and the questions and think about if they learned their lesson or not," Daniel Caldwell, 14, of Gulfport says of jury duty. "If you think they haven't, you give them a lot of punishment."

Once the jury reaches its verdict, the judge hands down the punishment. If the defendant completes the sentence, his record is wiped clean. If not, the case may be sent back to a professional court.

TOUGH PUNISHMENT

There isn't any jail time here, but teen court isn't taken lightly.

"Kids can impose some tough sentences," Mr. Fredericks says. "Sometimes they are tougher than a juvenile court judge."

A boy who shoplifted from a store had to write an apology on 1,000 index cards and hand each card to people entering the store. Another got 60 hours of community service on the beach, but he didn't have time to go swimming—he had to clean every men's restroom there.

The point, teen court coordinators say, is that the program works.

In Harrison County's regular juvenile court, 40 percent of first-time offenders will appear in court again. In Harrison County Teen Court, however, only 3 percent become repeat offenders.

"We change some lives here," executive director Fredericks says.

LEARNING THE LAW

Michael Swanier, 15, of Gulfport wants to be a prosecutor. (He and Joey Robinson are members of BSA[1] Explorer Post 2310, run by the Gulfport Police Department.) Boyd is considering a career as a criminal attorney. Daniel Caldwell has always been interested in the law.

Teen court helps them learn.

"You're dealing with different types of crimes," Michael says, "and you learn that it's not always a pretty world. It's a good program. You learn what other teens think about and how you can help them straighten up."

1 **BSA:** Boy Scouts of America. This article first appeared in *Boy's Life*, a magazine published by the Boy Scouts organization.

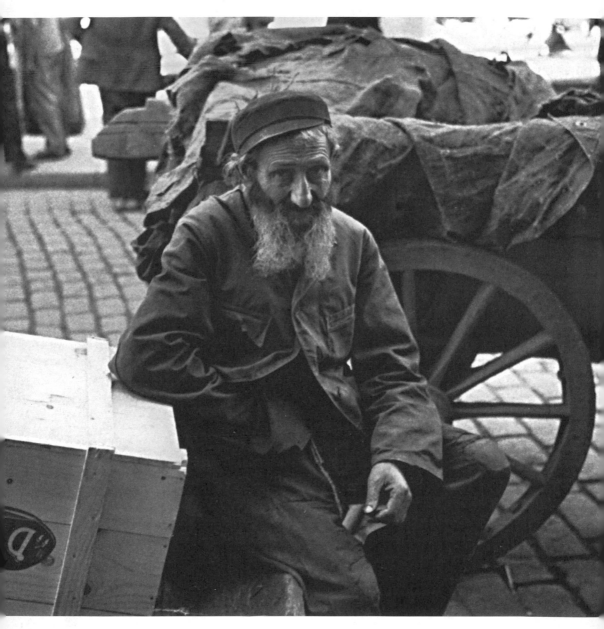

A PORTER AT REST 1937 Roman Vishniac

Shrewd Todie and Lyzer the Miser

Isaac Bashevis Singer

In a village somewhere in the Ukraine there lived a poor man called Todie. Todie had a wife, Shaindel, and seven children, but he could never earn enough to feed them properly. He tried many trades and failed in all of them. It was said of Todie that if he decided to deal in candles the sun would never set. He was nicknamed Shrewd Todie because whenever he managed to make some money, it was always by trickery.

This winter was an especially cold one. The snowfall was heavy and Todie had no money to buy wood for the stove. His seven children stayed in bed all day to keep warm. When the frost burns outside, hunger is stronger than ever, but Shaindel's larder[1] was empty. She reproached Todie bitterly, wailing, "If you can't feed your wife and children, I will go to the rabbi and get a divorce."

"And what will you do with it, eat it?" Todie retorted.

In the same village there lived a rich man called Lyzer. Because of his stinginess he was known as Lyzer the Miser. He permitted his wife to bake bread only once in four weeks because he had discovered that fresh bread is eaten up more quickly than stale.

Todie had more than once gone to Lyzer for a loan of a few gulden,[2] but Lyzer had always replied: "I sleep better when the money lies in my strongbox rather than in your pocket."

Lyzer had a goat, but he never fed her. The goat had learned to visit the houses of the neighbors, who pitied her and gave her potato peelings.

1 **larder:** food pantry

2 **gulden:** unit of money equal to 100 cents

Sometimes, when there were not enough peelings, she would gnaw on the old straw of the thatched roofs. She also had a liking for tree bark. Nevertheless, each year the goat gave birth to a kid. Lyzer milked her but, miser that he was, did not drink the milk himself. Instead he sold it to others.

Todie decided that he would take revenge on Lyzer and at the same time make some much-needed money for himself.

One day, as Lyzer was sitting on a box eating borscht[3] and dry bread (he used his chairs only on holidays so that the upholstery would not wear out), the door opened and Todie came in.

"Reb Lyzer," he said, "I would like to ask you a favor. My oldest daughter, Basha, is already fifteen and she's about to become engaged. A young man is coming from Janev[4] to look her over. My cutlery is tin, and my wife is ashamed to ask the young man to eat soup with a tin spoon. Would you lend me one of your silver spoons? I give you my holy word that I will return it to you tomorrow."

Lyzer knew that Todie would not dare to break a holy oath and he lent him the spoon.

No young man came to see Basha that evening. As usual, the girl walked around barefoot and in rags, and the silver spoon lay hidden under Todie's shirt. In the early years of his marriage Todie had possessed a set of silver tableware himself. He had, however, long since sold it all, with the exception of three silver teaspoons that were used only on Passover.

The following day, as Lyzer, his feet bare (in order to save his shoes), sat on his box eating borscht and dry bread, Todie returned.

"Here is the spoon I borrowed yesterday," he said, placing it on the table together with one of his own teaspoons.

"What is the teaspoon for?" Lyzer asked.

And Todie said: "Your tablespoon gave birth to a teaspoon. It is her child. Since I am an honest man, I'm returning both mother and child to you."

Lyzer looked at Todie in astonishment. He had never heard of a silver spoon giving birth to another. Nevertheless, his greed overcame his doubt and he happily accepted both spoons. Such an unexpected piece of good fortune! He was overjoyed that he had loaned Todie the spoon.

A few days later, as Lyzer (without his coat, to save it) was again sitting

3 **borscht:** soup made primarily of beets

4 **Janev:** a town in the Ukraine

on his box eating borscht with dry bread, the door opened and Todie appeared.

"The young man from Janev did not please Basha because he had donkey ears, but this evening another young man is coming to look her over. Shaindel is cooking soup for him, but she's ashamed to serve him with a tin spoon. Would you lend me . . ."

Even before Todie could finish the sentence, Lyzer interrupted. "You want to borrow a silver spoon? Take it with pleasure."

The following day Todie once more returned the spoon and with it one of his own silver teaspoons. He again explained that during the night the large spoon had given birth to a small one and in all good conscience he was bringing back the mother and newborn baby. As for the young man who had come to look Basha over, she hadn't liked him either, because his nose was so long that it reached to his chin. Needless to say that Lyzer the Miser was overjoyed.

Exactly the same thing happened a third time. Todie related that this time his daughter had rejected her suitor because he stammered. He also reported that Lyzer's silver spoon had again given birth to a baby spoon.

"Does it ever happen that a spoon has twins?" Lyzer inquired.

Todie thought it over for a moment. "Why not? I've even heard of a case where a spoon had triplets."

Almost a week passed by and Todie did not go to see Lyzer. But on Friday morning, as Lyzer (in his underdrawers to save his pants) sat on his box eating borscht and dry bread, Todie came in and said, "Good day to you, Reb Lyzer."

"A good morning and many more to you," Lyzer replied in his friendliest manner. "What good fortune brings you here? Did you perhaps come to borrow a silver spoon? If so, help yourself."

"Today I have a very special favor to ask. This evening a young man from the big city of Lublin is coming to look Basha over. He is the son of a rich man and I'm told he is clever and handsome as well. Not only do I need a silver spoon, but since he will remain with us over the Sabbath I need a pair of silver candlesticks, because mine are brass and my wife is ashamed to place them on the Sabbath table. Would you lend me your candlesticks? Immediately after the Sabbath, I will return them to you."

Silver candlesticks are of great value and Lyzer the Miser hesitated, but only for a moment.

Remembering his good fortune with the spoons, he said: "I have eight silver candlesticks in my house. Take them all. I know you will return them to me just as you say. And if it should happen that any of them give birth, I have no doubt that you will be as honest as you have been in the past."

"Certainly," Todie said. "Let's hope for the best."

The silver spoon, Todie hid beneath his shirt as usual. But taking the candlesticks, he went directly to a merchant, sold them for a considerable sum, and brought the money to Shaindel. When Shaindel saw so much money, she demanded to know where he had gotten such a treasure.

"When I went out, a cow flew over our roof and dropped a dozen silver eggs," Todie replied. "I sold them and here is the money."

"I have never heard of a cow flying over a roof and laying silver eggs," Shaindel said doubtingly.

"There is always a first time," Todie answered. "If you don't want the money, give it back to me."

"There'll be no talk about giving it back," Shaindel said. She knew that her husband was full of cunning and tricks—but when the children are hungry and the larder is empty, it is better not to ask too many questions. Shaindel went to the marketplace and bought meat, fish, white flour, and even some nuts and raisins for a pudding. And since a lot of money still remained, she bought shoes and clothes for the children.

It was a very gay Sabbath in Todie's house. The boys sang and the girls danced. When the children asked their father where he had gotten the money, he replied: "It is forbidden to mention money during the Sabbath."

Sunday, as Lyzer (barefoot and almost naked to save his clothes) sat on his box finishing up a dry crust of bread with borscht, Todie arrived and, handing him his silver spoon, said, "It's too bad. This time your spoon did not give birth to a baby."

"What about the candlesticks?" Lyzer inquired anxiously.

Todie sighed deeply. "The candlesticks died."

Lyzer got up from his box so hastily that he overturned his plate of borscht.

"You fool! How can candlesticks die?" he screamed.

"If spoons can give birth, candlesticks can die."

Lyzer raised a great hue and cry and had Todie called before the rabbi. When the rabbi heard both sides of the story, he burst out laughing. "It serves you right," he said to Lyzer. "If you hadn't chosen to believe that spoons give birth, now you would not be forced to believe that your candlesticks died."

"But it's all nonsense," Lyzer objected.

"Did you not expect the candlesticks to give birth to other candlesticks?" the rabbi said admonishingly. "If you accept nonsense when it brings you profit, you must also accept nonsense when it brings you loss." And he dismissed the case.

The following day, when Lyzer the Miser's wife brought him his borscht and dry bread, Lyzer said to her, "I will eat only the bread. Borscht is too expensive a food, even without sour cream."

The story of the silver spoons that gave birth and the candlesticks that died spread quickly through the town. All the people enjoyed Todie's victory and Lyzer the Miser's defeat. The shoemaker's and tailor's apprentices, as was their custom whenever there was an important happening, made up a song about it:

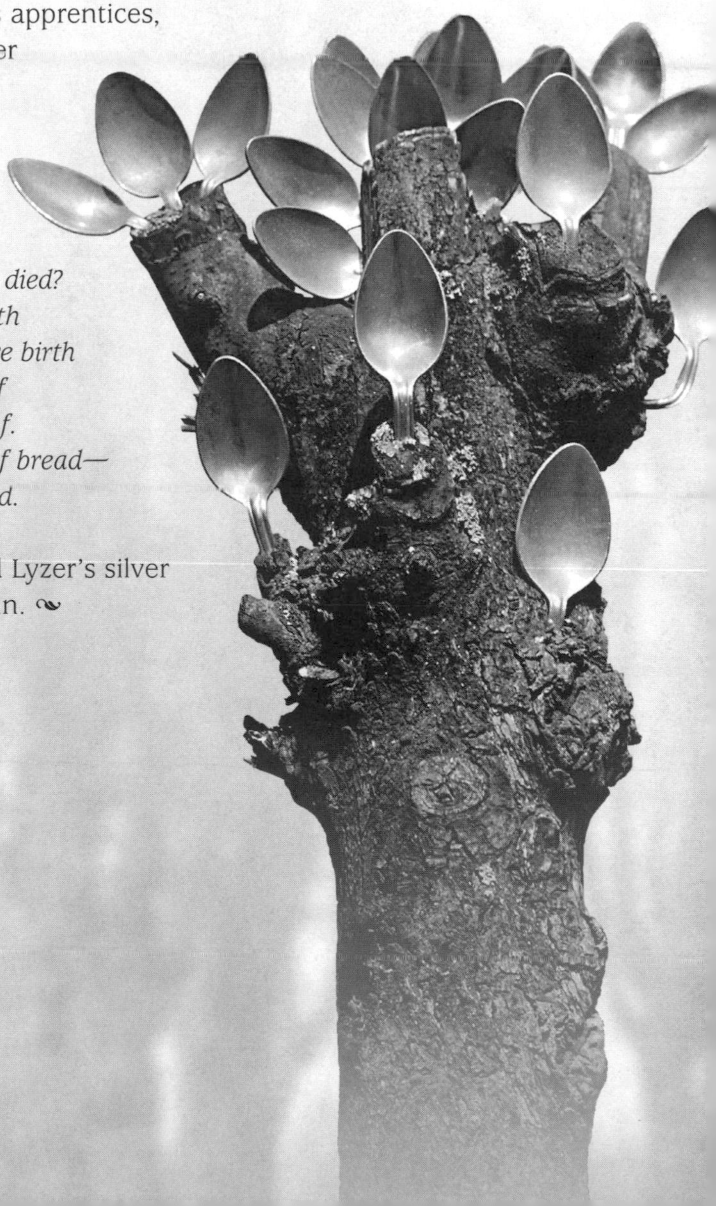

Lyzer, put your grief aside.
What if your candlesticks have died?
You're the richest man on earth
With silver spoons that can give birth
And silver eggs as living proof
Of flying cows above your roof.
Don't sit there eating crusts of bread—
To silver grandsons look ahead.

However, time passed and Lyzer's silver spoons never gave birth again. ∾

justice

w. r. rodriguez

a youth grabbed an old woman's purse fat with tissues and aspirin and such sundries[1] as old women carry in sagging purses a desperate youth nice enough not to beat her head bloody into the sidewalk as muggers of the feeble often do for the fun of it i suppose and he ran up the hill but one of the perennial watchers watched it all from her window the purseless old woman in slow pursuit yelling such curses as it takes old women a lifetime to learn but it was too dangerous too futile the silent watcher knew to call the police who might come and rough up someone they did not like just for the fun of it i suppose or who would talk polite and feel mad inside and roll their eyes because there was really nothing they could do and there were murders and assaults to handle so this silent angry watcher carelessly but carefully dropped flower pots from her fourth floor windowsill garden one crashing before one behind and the third hitting him on the head a geranium i suppose and closed her window while the huffing grateful old woman looked up at the heavens to thank the lord and walked off with her purse laughing when she finally calmed down and leaving the youth to awaken in the blue arms of the law and do you know two smiling cops walked up all those stairs to warn the watcher that if she weren't more careful with her plants she would get a ticket for littering i suppose

1 **sundries:** miscellaneous items

Words

Dian Curtis Regan

Mellisa Meeker tapped on the door of her brother's bedroom. "Are you ready? Dad's bringing the car around."

No answer.

She peeked inside. Andy slumped on the edge of his bed, tie dangling from one hand, head resting in the other.

"Andy?"

He didn't move.

Puzzled, Mellisa stepped into the room. "Hey, big brother, what's wrong? Your fans await you. The whole town's coming to see its fave young writer receive the Tabor Medal."

She waited for Andy's typical smug smile, but he ignored her pep talk.

Whoa. This isn't the brother I know and envy.

She sat beside him. "Hey, Famous Senior." Flattery always worked.

Andy pulled his hand from his face. He looked awful—dark hair mussed, face red and splotchy.

Mellisa drew back. Had her self-assured brother been crying? "What? Are you nervous? The great orator of the Meeker family? Captain of the Whitman High Debate team? I could no more give an acceptance speech than—"

"Go."

His sharp response bit off the end of her sentence.

"Hey, it's me. I know your secrets and you know mine." She waited for him to acknowledge the reference to their late-night bonding sessions after Mom died. Dad had his own grief to deal with. All she and Andy had were each other—alone in the tiny apartment on the wrong side of town.

"*Leave*," he insisted. "Tell Dad I'm riding to school with Jackson."

"Fine." Mellisa stepped to the door, hiding hurt feelings, waiting for him to grin at her and say, *Hey, I'm sorry. Case of nerves, that's all.*

But he didn't.

She strode down the dark-paneled corridor to the curved oak staircase, unable to descend this magnificent stairway without gliding down, pretending to be one of the many distinguished women who'd visited this mansion in years past. The mansion her family of the tiny apartment now called home.

At the bottom, she reverted back to Mellisa Meeker, daughter of Andrew Meeker III, granddaughter of Andrew Meeker II.

Andrew the second had built Meeker Mansion in the sixties. Oil money. That was the simple version of how her grandfather came into his fortune.

Mellisa pounded across the marble foyer and out the double front doors. Her father's rusty '89 Jeep idled in the curved drive. The Cadillac, inherited from his father, remained in the five-car garage.

Mellisa slid inside. "Andy's riding with Jackson," she explained.

Nodding, her father, the rebellious heir to the throne, released the emergency brake and took off.

Mellisa studied his profile as they rode along the quiet streets of Sinclair Hills. He acted annoyed at the posh neighborhood, insulted that his father had bequeathed[1] him the mansion as well as a board position at Meeker Oil. Not what the anti-establishment, long-haired hippie, "I'm never going to be like you when I grow up" son had envisioned for a career. He'd done okay working for an environmental recycling firm until *downsizing* became a key word in the industry. How could a single dad—out of work with kids to support—remain a rebel?

"Look at all the cars," Dad exclaimed as they neared Whitman High. "This town sure comes out on award night to support its local sports heros."

Mellisa spotted the Channel 9 van. A satellite dish perched on top like a party hat. Even though most of the audience was here to cheer for Whitman's star athletes, she was proud of Andy for his literary win.

Shuddering at the sight of the news team and camera, Mellisa braced herself as Dad zigzagged into a parking spot. How could Andy address hundreds of people with a TV camera in his face? She would have melted into a puddle of self-consciousness.

1 **bequeathed:** willed; left as in a last will and testament

Mellisa climbed from the Jeep. "I could *never* be the center of attention like Andy. I'm warning you, Dad, I won't amount to much."

She watched him lock the door, wondering how he felt about Andy being the perfect conformist son *his* father had wanted.

"Sure you will, Mell."

"Nope. Never going to win a Pulitzer or Nobel if it involves public speaking. Won't even try."

"Ha. I'm glad my daughter sets high goals for herself."

Mellisa looped an arm through his as they walked, marveling at the number of people streaming toward the auditorium.

Too bad Grandpa couldn't be here tonight. As a self-made man, he'd made up for his lack of education by filling Meeker Mansion with books—*three* libraries, plus a volume-filled garret[2] above the east wing where he retreated whenever he wearied of being an oil baron.

How proud Grandpa would've been to know that Andrew Meeker IV had written a prize-winning collection of poems and prose in his beloved garret.

Mellisa often browsed the many bookshelves, but found no romances or science fiction adventures, just lots of biographies, history books, and classics—far too much *lit-tra-chure* for her taste.

Andy loved the libraries—probably because he'd wanted to be an author ever since fourth grade, when he wrote a goofy parody[3] of " 'Twas the Night Before Christmas" ("and all through the school, not a student was working or obeying a rule. . . .") The impressed teacher circulated copies—and Andy's reputation as a writer was launched.

▲ ▲ ▲

Mellisa led her father into the auditorium. Mrs. Castano, the history teacher who'd taught at Whitman for at least a hundred years, was instantly beside them. "There you are," she exclaimed. "Seats for the award recipients and their families are down front."

Down front? Cool.

"Where is . . . ?" Mrs. Castano dipped her head to peer at the incoming crowd over her reading glasses.

"Andy's riding with a friend," Dad explained. "He'll be here in a minute."

2 **garret:** small attic
3 **parody:** a comical imitation

Nodding, Mrs. Castano escorted them down the slanted aisle toward the stage. Part of Mellisa wished Andy was with them so everyone would recognize her as the Wonder Boy's sister. Another part was glad he wasn't. It let her be the anonymous sophomore that she was.

Front row left. Roped-off seats. Impressive.

Letter jacketed jocks filled the rest of the front row. Already they were rowdy, ignoring Mrs. Castano's pleas to tone it down.

Mellisa studied the awards program: Welcome from Principal Osaka. Music by the Senior Chorale. Presentation of awards to the newspaper staff and outstanding members of various school clubs. *Then*, presentation of the Tabor Medal (to Andy!). Lastly, sports awards to the hotshots of Whitman High.

Ha, they saved the loudest awards for last.

Onstage, Mr. Sampson, the English lit teacher, was testing the microphone and acting self-important. In the orchestra pit, Ms. Tooley hustled band members to their places.

Where was Andy? Mellisa twisted in her seat to scan the aisles. It was almost time for the program to begin.

Feeling nervous for him made it hard to sit still. She tugged on Dad's sleeve to interrupt his chat with Andy's trig teacher. "I'm going to get a drink."

Out in the main hall, somebody thumped her on the head.

"Jackson, there you are." Mellisa gazed up at her brother's best friend. All six feet four inches of him. "Where's Andy?"

Jackson's dark eyes glinted. "He came with you."

Confused, she pictured Andy in his room, disheveled and depressed. Alarm made her clutch Jackson's sleeve. "No he didn't."

Jackson's amusement turned to concern. He jiggled his car keys. "Let's go get him."

Mellisa ran to keep up with Jackson's lanky strides. She *should* go back to tell Dad they were leaving, but the look on Andy's face when he'd ordered her from his room spurred her on.

Something must be terribly wrong.

▲ ▲ ▲

The mansion was dark. Mellisa and Jackson raced through the foyer and up the stairs, clicking on lights as they ran.

Andy's room was empty. Mellisa's heart pounded as she snatched his crumpled tie from the floor.

"Meeker!" Jackson shouted down the hallway. "You here?"

Creaking from the thirty-year-old mansion was their only answer.

Jackson moved down the hall, opening doors to make sure every room was empty. "Why would he bolt, Mell? He craves the spotlight."

"I don't know." Fear made her voice tremble. She hated anything that upset her life. Mom. A new home. A new school. Too, too much.

Andy, what are you doing?

She followed Jackson down the hall, absently winding her brother's tie around her hand. "Did Andy say anything strange to you or act different?"

Jackson shrugged. "He gets moody sometimes. Who doesn't?"

The panicky feeling that consumed her after Mom died tightened Mellisa's chest. "We've got to find him," she said.

Jackson headed for the stairs. "You look up here. I'll search the main floor, and—"

"No."

"But you said—"

"There's only one place Andy could be."

Turning, Mellisa ran upstairs to the third-floor guest rooms. Jackson was on her heels. At the end of the hallway, she opened a narrow door, exposing a curved stairwell, paneled in dark mahogany.

She flipped on a light. The bulb blinked out with a foreboding *pop*.

"Where do these stairs go?" Jackson whispered.

"To my grandfather's garret."

Stumbling on the first step, Mellisa stopped. "Um, I need to go up alone."

"But why?"

"I—I just need to." Loyalty to her brother kicked in, making her want to protect his ego. He never cried in front of anyone—not even at Mom's funeral. And only once in front of his little sister.

"Look," she began. "I know you guys are friends, but . . ." Hesitating, Mellisa tried to be tactful. "If Andy's up there, I think he'll be straight with me. If you're there, he may clam up. It's a guy thing, you know?"

Jackson looked wounded but stepped back as if he understood. Reaching into his pocket, he handed her a key chain. "Here's a flashlight in case you need it."

Mellisa crept up the dark stairway, aiming the mini-light at the steps. She'd been to the garret only once. At first she had thought she'd like the round room, because it reminded her of a high tower in a castle. But the floor to ceiling windows unnerved her. Beyond a narrow ledge was a sheer, four-story drop. Made her nervous. She'd never gone up there again.

Didn't bother Andy. He loved the garret enough to turn it into his writing room.

At the top of the circular stairs, a soft glow outlined the door. Clicking off the flashlight, Mellisa stepped inside, letting her eyes adjust to the dim lamplight. Her heart skittered when she realized the garret was empty.

A movement drew her attention to the far window.

Andy. Outside, sitting on the ledge.

Mellisa sucked in a breath. There was nothing between him and the concrete drive far below.

She moved slowly, not wanting to startle him.

"I knew you'd come back," he said dully, not bothering to turn around.

Mellisa's heart stalled. "Why are you out there?"

Twisting sideways, he scowled. "I think even a lowly sophomore can figure out why I'm out here."

"Touché,"[4] she muttered.

It was an old joke between them: lowly sophomores, conceited seniors. But this time, it wasn't funny.

She stopped three feet from the window. "Come inside," she demanded. Her fear of heights was new—sparked by images of her mother falling off a mountain to her death. The similarity of her brother's apparent intentions seemed beyond cruel.

"Why are you doing this to us?" *To me*, is what she really meant.

In the faint light, Andy's face scrunched in pain. "I'm not doing anything *to you*."

Anger heated her neck. Forget not showing up at school or not accepting his award. How *dare* he think of throwing himself off the mansion tower? How dare he think it would not affect her? Or Dad?

Her mind flashed back to the horrifying news from Alpine State Park where Mom had worked during tourist season. How her crampons[5] had slipped on the sheer face of a cliff. How a rope had been tied improperly.

Falling.

Mellisa couldn't breathe. "Andy, why?"

4 **touché:** French word used to acknowledge a point; pronounced "to-shay"

5 **crampons:** climbing spikes used on mountaineering footwear

"It's in the note," he blurted, motioning toward the desk.

Mellisa spotted the envelope on Grandpa's ink blotter. Dropping Andy's tie onto the desk, she opened the letter:

To the ones I leave behind,
The ones I hold most dear.
Remember me in softer times,
With friends and family near.

Before her mind could question if this mindless Hallmarky twaddle[6] was the best he could do to say a permanent good-bye to his family, her gaze fell upon a line at the bottom of the page:

"*Even these words are not my own, but Donovan Mueller's.*"

Mellisa glanced up at him, confused. "This doesn't tell me anything.'

Exasperated, Andy swung around to sit sideways on the ledge.

Good, Mellisa told herself. *Talk him back inside.*

"Read between the lines!"

Mellisa flinched. Andy never yelled. She forced herself to stay calm. "Who is Donovan Mueller?"

"Look it up," he hissed.

With a sarcastic *tsk*ing, she motioned at the hundreds of volumes surrounding her. "So, where do I start?"

Cursing at her, Andy grasped the window frame and pulled himself inside.

6 **Hallmarky twaddle:** silly, shallow words such as those found on some greeting cards

Relief loosened the white-knuckled grip of her clasped hands.

Andy walked the stacks, trailing his fingers along book spines. Stopping, he yanked out the title he was searching for and flung it at her.

Mellisa dove to catch the heavy book, then flipped to the index. "Mueller, Donovan, page 1365." Finding the page, she scanned his bio. "He's an eighteenth-century writer. So what?"

"Look further."

She looked. "To the Ones I Leave Behind." Closing the book, Mellisa studied her brother's tense face. "You borrowed this guy's suicide note?"

"Think, Mell. I stole another writer's words."

"But you put his name on it."

Andy scoffed. "Yeah. *This* time I did."

The meaning of his words sank in. "You mean . . . the poems and stories you wrote for the Tabor competition? You borrowed words from other authors?"

Hanging his head, Andy turned away. "Borrowed. Stole. Same thing."

"How could you? You're a great writer. You don't have to—"

He waved a hand to silence her. Agitated, he paced across the garret, shirttail out. "I choked, Mell. Everybody expected me to win. Sampson was afraid some girl from Easton was going to take the medal. It's been six years since a Whitman student won. He was on some kind of mission. Kept hounding me. And . . . and I *tried*. But everything I wrote was drivel.[7] I couldn't even show it to him."

While Andy talked, Mellisa casually circled the garret and lowered the window, careful not to look out. His words edged guilt into her mind. *How could I not have noticed that something was wrong?*

He's a good actor.

Andy straightened the reading lamp with a shaky hand. "Then there's Dad."

His voice quivered so much, Mellisa barely caught his words.

Andy glanced at her, as if hoping she wasn't listening. "Dad's already been humiliated by swallowing his pride and accepting Grandpa's inheritance. Plus losing Mom. How could I let him down by not winning?"

"*Forget* winning. How could you let him down by *cheating*?"

Mellisa knew her words were cruel, but she was angry.

He took the insult without flinching. "Touché, Sis. The deal is—no one would ever suspect that I cheated. But I did. I lied to Dad and Sampson.

7 **drivel:** nonsense; writing of no literary value

Told them I was working on something so great no one could read it until I was finished. Truth is, I wrote nothing until the night before it was due."

The memory came back to Mellisa. "You stayed up here that night. I thought you'd fallen asleep."

"No, I pulled an all-nighter. Wrote the poems and stories for the almighty Tabor Committee. For Dad and Mr. Sampson." He gestured at the bookshelves. "I figured if I stole words verbatim from successful but dead obscure authors, I might be able to fool everybody."

Mellisa couldn't believe what she was hearing. "And?"

He shrugged. "Well, it worked. Nobody noticed."

"Yet," Mellisa added.

Andy shoved the reference book back into place on the shelf. "You're right. I'd live in fear that someday I'd be exposed."

He slumped into a chair. "I guess you could also call me a coward. Look what Dad did when he was my age. Turned down his father's money and left home just to be true to his own beliefs. And me? I caved."

Reaching across the desk, he slammed a notebook shut to punctuate his comment. "At least Dad's choice let him sleep at night. Mine is a prison—as long as I live."

As long as I live echoed in Mellisa's head. She blocked unpleasant images from her mind's eye.

"Remember the poem Sampson loved about the girl who followed the sailor to sea?" Andy continued.

Mellisa remembered.

"I stole it from a guy named William Anthony Tyndale, who can't sue me because he's been dead for two hundred years."

"Oh, Andy, your reputation—"

"Is shot," he finished. "I thought I could go on stage, accept the award, make Sampson happy, make my dad proud, then never do this again, but . . ." With sudden anger, he shoved a stack of papers off the desk.

Mellisa watched the pages flutter to the patterned carpet. "I think it's *good* you've had an attack of conscience."

He glowered at her. "Easy for you to say. You don't have an auditorium filled with people waiting to applaud a success that isn't yours."

Mellisa glanced at her watch. The program was well underway. Mrs. Castano was probably pacing the parking lot, searching for Andy, while keeping his absence a secret from Mr. Sampson, whose temper was best avoided.

Somewhere on a floor below, a phone rang. Had to be Dad. Ready to send out a search party for his kids.

Andy came to his feet. "Who answered the phone?"

"Relax, it's only Jackson." Mellisa was glad Jackson was there to catch the phone and explain things to Dad as best he could. Taking a breath, she plunged on. "Let's go."

Andy gave her an incredulous look. "Go where?"

"To school. You've got unfinished business."

Surprise and fear shadowed his face in the lamplight. "Are you crazy? I can't go on stage and pretend—"

"You're not going to."

"What do you mean?" He studied her face. "Ho, wait a minute. You want me to go up there and confess? Tell everyone I plagiarized the winning entry in the Tabor competition? Tell everyone I'm a fraud?"

By the end of the questions, he was screaming at her.

"Yes, Andrew James Meeker the fourth. You have a way with words. You'll think of something to say while we're driving."

"Words." He spat it out like a curse. "They're only words."

Opening the door, Mellisa motioned for him to follow.

"Hey, wait!" Andy yanked her away from the stairwell. "Five minutes ago, I was about to jump off the damn ledge. If you hadn't shown up when you did, I'd . . . I'd . . ."

"Still be sitting there." Remembering Andy's tie, Mellisa rescued it from the desk and wrapped it around his neck, tucking it beneath his collar. He stood quietly, acting defeated, letting her smooth his hair and fumble with the tie. "I know you too well. You would *not* end your life just to save face."

A tear escaped from the corner of his eye. He slashed at his cheek with one hand, acting annoyed that emotions would betray him. "So you think I don't have enough guts to let go of the ledge?"

Not answering, she flubbed the knot on his tie for the third time.

Pushing her hands away, he tied it himself.

"Facing everyone at school will require all the guts you can muster."

Mellisa was suddenly aware of Jackson shuffling in the stairwell. How long had he been listening?

Andy turned away, hugging himself the way he used to when he was little and something had scared him. "I can't do it, Mell. I can't face them."

She touched his shoulder. "Yes, you can. You've been on that stage before, Mr. Debate Captain. You know how to win an audience over with words."

He scoffed. "This is different. What words do I offer tonight? How I've let Whitman down? Why I can't accept the honor?"

She held his gaze for a long moment. "Couldn't have said it better myself."

He pointed a finger at her. "I'll get even for this, little sister."

He said it in jest, but she knew he meant it. "Touché," she answered.

▲ ▲ ▲

The auditorium was dark when they arrived. Teresa Fuji was playing a flute solo. Teresa always played flute solos, but Mellisa didn't remember her being on tonight's program. Some rearranging must have been done to stall for the belated arrival of one of the award recipients.

Mrs Castano, stationed in the hall, waved the instant she spotted them, then flew to the stage door to alert Mr. Sampson.

"Jackson and I will sit in back," Andy whispered. "Tell Dad we're here."

Great. I get to walk down the aisle while someone's performing.

Keeping her eyes focused on the footlights, Mellisa hurried toward the stage. Hunching over, she scuttled to her seat.

Dad greeted her with a flurry of whispered questions.

She calmed him down, promising to explain later.

Mellisa sat stiffly, applauding for Teresa and her flute. As the lights came up, she noticed that the athletes were clutching trophies. So. The sports awards were over. Andy must be last.

Mr. Sampson strode across the stage. His furrowed brow didn't tell Mellisa anything, since his brow was always furrowed.

He harrumphed a few times into the microphone and glared at the audience like he did at every assembly. Mellisa expected him to act differently when parents were present, but he never did.

The teacher began by thanking the audience for allowing him to rearrange the order of presentations. Then he launched into the history of the Tabor Medal, how it had been inspired by a talented student back in the seventies who went on to write for the theater and now funded the citywide award: an engraved cut-glass paperweight for the winner, plus two thousand dollars for the winning school's library.

Mr. Sampson spoke glowingly of this year's winner, making sure the audience knew that *he* was Andy's lit teacher, as though taking credit for the win.

A few chuckles rippled through the crowd. Mellisa didn't think Mr. Sampson had meant for his bragging to be funny.

During the rave introduction, pride flickered on her father's face.

Groaning, Mellisa squirmed in her seat. The next ten minutes promised to be excruciating.

Applause carried her brother down the aisle and onto the stage. His tie was on straight, his sports jacket buttoned, and his hair combed. He looked like the same confident brother Mellisa had seen on stage before.

Her hands began to shake in empathy.[8] She'd die if that many people were staring at her, waiting for her to speak.

Andy waited for the applause to die down. He opened a wrinkled paper clutched in his hands and smoothed it onto the podium.

"Before I begin," he said, "I'd like to ask my sister, Mellisa Meeker, to join me up here at the podium."

His words stopped Mellisa's breath. *What's he doing*!? *This has nothing to do with me. He knows I can't go up there.*

Andy shaded his eyes with one hand and peered into the audience. Dad nudged her. "Hey, Mell, he wants to share his moment of glory with his sister. Go on up."

"Mellisa?" Andy spoke her name slowly, the way he said it whenever he was doing something to get even.

She knew. She knew what he was doing. Since she was making him face his biggest fear, and not taking *no* for an answer, he was making her do the same. Face her own fear. Her biggest nightmare.

The audience began to applaud—to speed things up, she figured. Suddenly Mrs. Castano was there, pulling her out of her seat. Being paralyzed, she couldn't have gotten to her feet any other way.

Andy, don't make me do this!

She gave him a desperate, pleading stare. Just hearing her name spoken into the microphone had already spun her heart out of control.

Mrs. Castano urged her toward the stairs, clutching her arm as if she sensed Mellisa was in a fight-or-flight mode.

Climbing the steps on shaky legs, she stood beside her brother, focusing on him instead of the audience. Or on all those eyes, staring at her.

Andy put one hand over the microphone and whispered, "Do I need to say, 'Touché'?"

"Shut up and give your damn speech. And don't you *dare* make me say anything."

He grinned at her. She could not grin back, yet his smile and the look in his eyes kept her knees from buckling. No, he wouldn't make her

8 **empathy:** sensitivity to another's feelings and experiences

speak. She knew he wasn't trying to be cruel. He needed her here.

He needed her.

Mellisa dared a glance at the audience. She couldn't see a thing! Thank God for the blinding brightness. Made her feel that she and Andy were here alone. The thought surged calmness through her. With the calmness came the sense that things would truly be all right.

Whitman High was about to receive its biggest shock of the year. People would gossip about the Meeker boy for weeks—months maybe. But eventually they'd turn to other topics, and this night would be forgotten.

"Friends, classmates, teachers, and guests," Andy began.

Mellisa's terrified heart overflowed with pride. Andy's voice was strong, like he owned the audience. As long as she focused on him and let the hazy cloud of footlights shield her, she was *almost* okay.

"I came here tonight to accept the Tabor Medal, given for excellence in writing."

Andy paused—a beat too long. Mellisa could hear the audience shifting, uncomfortable at the extended silence.

"I am declining this prestigious award."

A collective gasp *whooshed* from the crowd.

Mellisa glanced offstage. A startled Mr. Sampson put a hand behind one ear as if he thought he hadn't heard correctly.

"The body of work I turned in for consideration by the Tabor Committee was not my own," Andy continued. "I know this was absolutely wrong. I cannot stand here and give you a valid excuse. I can only say that I could not live with myself if I perpetrated this dishonest act."

Facing Mr. Sampson, he said, "Sir, I am truly sorry." Squinting beyond the footlights, he added, "Dad? I ask your forgiveness."

The silence in the auditorium was much louder than the thunderous applause had been after Andy's introduction.

Stepping back from the podium, he held out a hand to Mellisa.

She grasped his hand, pleased that he knew she'd never make it across the stage and down the steps without someone to hold onto. "You chose the perfect words," she whispered.

He shrugged, as if turning down awards was a nightly habit. Holding her hand like a lifeline, he led her off stage. Mellisa realized for the first time that the lifeline ran both directions. Her overly confident brother needed her as much as she-of-little-confidence needed him. Go figure.

Mellisa fully expected Andy to keep on going—right out the emergency exit and far away from this place.

But he didn't.

He led her back to the seats in the front row.

She tried to read her father's face, but it was a strange mixture of sadness and awe.

Rising, Dad put his arms around his son, holding him in silence.

Mellisa hung back, hating the way this private moment was being witnessed. It reminded her of Mom's funeral, how Dad had broken down in front of everyone, and how she couldn't bear to see him like that.

How she'd fled to get away from staring eyes, and how Andy had come looking for her. Hiding in a juniper grove in Alpine Park in freezing rain, they'd cried together.

For a long moment no one in the auditorium moved or spoke. Then Mr. Sampson stepped to the microphone. Mellisa could tell he was shaken, because he wasn't scowling as usual. His expression surprised her. It was not one of disappointment, but of astonishment.

"Before I turn the program back to Principal Osaka, I'd like to say that the short speech we've just heard must have caused Andy Meeker a great deal of pain to deliver. I cannot applaud Mr. Meeker on the actions he has confessed. But I can applaud him on his honesty in stopping the lie."

Andy began to tremble. The difficult part was over. Mellisa figured his brain must have just kicked in. Dad kept one arm firmly around his son's shoulders.

"Andy," Mr. Sampson finished. "I implore you to put tonight's experience behind you. But tomorrow. Ah, tomorrow and tomorrow and tomorrow, I . . . we—the entire community of Whitman High—we expect great things from you."

No one applauded. It would have been a perfect ending, but Mellisa knew applause would let Andy off the hook too easily. His punishment wasn't over. He still had to face everyone—in the halls and on the street. That, too, would take guts.

The Meeker family sat down to wait out the closing song by the Whitman Senior Chorale. "The Long and Winding Road."

How appropriate, Mellisa thought.

Andy nudged her. His face was pale, but a spark still glinted in his eyes. "And I," he whispered, "expect great things from you, Mellisa Emily Meeker the first."

"You got it," she told him. "I'll say *anything* to make you happy. After all, they're only *words*."

She knew his response before he said it.

"Touché."

Responding to Cluster Two

Who judges?

Thinking Skill ANALYZING

1. State your opinion on the peer court system for trying youthful offenders. Do you feel it is effective and appropriate?
2. "Shrewd Todie and Lyzer the Miser" has a clear *moral*, best summed up in the judge's final statement: "If you accept nonsense when it brings you profit, you must also accept nonsense when it brings you loss." **Analyze** the other three selections in this cluster and write a *moral* that best states the theme of each piece.
3. The phrase "i suppose" is repeated several times in the poem, "justice." Why do you think w. r. rodriguez uses this poetic technique?
4. In "Words," suppose that as punishment Andy had to speak in schools on the topic of plagiarism. What do you suppose he would discuss? Write an outline of at least three main points you think Andy would cover in his talks.

Writing Activity: Here Comes the Judge

Pretend that the position of juvenile court judge is open at your courthouse. Write a job description for this position.

A Strong Job Description

- states the duties of the job
- lists the character traits desired
- details prior experience and education preferred
- describes the rewards of the job

CLUSTER THREE

Punishment or Mercy?

Thinking Skill COMPARING AND CONTRASTING

UN MARCHAND D'ORANGES 1848 Eugène Delacroix

The Quality of Mercy

RETOLD BY SHARON CREEDEN
(MOROCCAN FOLK TALE)

In ancient times, in Morocco and in the city of Casablanca,[1] there was a rich and prominent merchant. One day the merchant fell ill and saw that he would not recover. He called for his only son and asked, "Son, what will you do with my money after I die?"

The son replied, "If anyone needs money, I will give him some. If anyone invites me to a party, I will go. What else is money for?"

The father groaned, "I should have taught you my business and how to make money grow. I was always too busy." The father died knowing that his fortune would be scattered to the winds.

And so it was, the son squandered his inheritance on gifts and celebrations. When he had no roof for his head or food for his belly, he went to the marketplace to beg alms.[2] He sat among the leather workers and the vegetable sellers with his outstretched hand. But on every corner were customers and friends of his father. He was ashamed to be seen begging. "I will go to Marrakesh.[3] No one knows me there," he told himself.

He walked barefoot from the coast of the Atlantic across the rising and falling waves of sand dunes. At last, rising out of the desert like a mirage, he saw the minaret[4] on the red ramparts[5] of Marrakesh. Behind the city

1 **Casablanca:** largest city in Morocco, a country in northwestern Africa

2 **alms:** money or food given to the poor

3 **Marrakesh:** another Moroccan city south of Casablanca

4 **minaret:** tall, thin tower of a mosque from which the call to prayer is chanted

5 **ramparts:** protective walls or embankments

towered the snowy range of the Atlas mountains. He walked through olive and palm groves into the city. "Surely I will find my fortune here," he thought.

But because he knew no work but begging, he was soon sitting in the square, surrounded by the music of cymbal and drum. The square was filled with fire-eaters, storytellers, watersellers, and traveling merchants.

One day, a man stopped and called the young beggar by name. "Is it you? Why are you begging?" He was a rich merchant and rival to his late father.

The young man was too ashamed to tell that he had spent his inheritance. Instead he lied. "I was traveling to buy goods! But thieves robbed me."

The rich merchant took pleasure in seeing his rival's son begging for coins. But he put on a kind face and said, "In your father's memory, I will help you. Come and share a glass of mint tea with me."

When they were seated on cushions inside the merchant's stall, the merchant made an astounding offer. "I shall lend you any sum you ask for. You can do whatever you wish with it; any profit you make will be yours. But there is a condition. If at the year's end you do not pay, I will cut one kilogram[6] of flesh from your body."

The young man was startled by the condition of the bargain. But he said, "I have no choice," and signed the agreement.

Throughout the year the young man engaged in business, but he was unlucky and untrained. He lost all the money. What did the young man do? At the end of the year, he went to the palace where the king sat in assembly. He sat outside the gates wringing his hands and rocking to and fro. He took no food or water and prayed he would die before his life was forfeit. He wept, "I should have been born a kitten and drowned at birth."

Days passed. Finally he was observed by the king's daughter. She was on her way to listen to the cases brought before her father. The Princess had a quick and clever mind, a tender heart, and a voice as sweet as a flute echoing through marble halls. Her mother and sisters stayed cloistered behind harem walls. Instead the Princess went to hear her father's judgments. She concealed herself in a room near the throne to listen to the proceedings. How wise and just was her father—always following the letter of the law.

So it was that one day the Princess saw the young man outside the gate, and she was touched by his despair. She sent her servant to ask,

6 **one kilogram:** unit of weight equal to just over two pounds

"Young man, why do you weep?"

It was not until the third day that the young man replied, "Because I was foolish, and tomorrow I shall die for it." He told his story. When the servant told the Princess, she sent a note which said, "Come to court tomorrow, and you will be aided by one who loves mercy."

The appointed hour came. The Princess disguised herself as a lawyer. She walked through arched corridors hung with silver lamps and entered the Royal Audience Chamber. The merchant and the young man were assembled with the crowds of petitioners. At last, the King asked the rich merchant, "What does the young man owe you?"

The merchant took the agreement out of his pocket. The King read it and asked the young man, "Do you agree that you signed this document?"

"Ruler of the stars, what can I say? You see my signature here. But one thing you must know. I entered into this agreement because I had no other choice."

Then the Princess stepped from the crowd. She was dressed in a hooded caftan[7] and kept her face turned and concealed in the hood. In a clear, strong voice, she addressed the King, "Our gracious lord! This was a bargain freely made. I agree, on behalf of my client, to give a kilogram of flesh to the merchant, but I insist that he cut off exactly one kilogram in a single stroke. If he cuts off too little, then he must make up the difference, and if he cuts off too much, he must restore the extra amount from his own body."

The merchant protested, "I demand justice!" I cannot cut exactly one kilogram of flesh in a single stroke. The agreement does not specify a single stroke."

"That is correct," the Princess said. "There is no such condition, but our most wise ruler, in his mercy, may impose one."

"Why should I impose a condition that is impossible, then the merchant is without his money or the flesh?" responded the King.

She answered his question, "The law would require that the merchant receive his payment, either money or flesh. Since there is no money, it is the flesh. And indeed, the merchant has come with a sharpened dagger beneath his robes. But where is the mercy in such a result? The young man will die; the merchant will have only a lump of flesh. And, you, my gracious lord, will have blood on your white marble floors."

7 **caftan:** an ankle-length, loose-fitting garment with long sleeves

She continued, "Perhaps there is another way, a way that provides justice and more kindness than justice requires."

The crowds were hushed and listening to the beardless young lawyer. The king leaned forward. "Counselor, would you enlighten us all about this other way."

"Yes, my lord. Let the merchant receive the labor of the young man until the debt is paid. The young man needs the guidance of a mentor.[8] The merchant needs to temper[9] his ethics with concern for more than money. All can gain from such a result."

"Well spoken!" replied the King. "And so it will be. Young debtor, use this opportunity to make something of yourself. Merchant, you shall take this young debtor into your service. Work and train him until the debt is discharged. It is our wish that you open your heart and mind to him, that you treat him as a son and bring him to the marketplace as a credit to you, his dead father, and your king."

The litigants[10] dropped to the floor and bowed to their king, arose and turned to leave the courtroom. As the crowd filed from the chamber, the King called to the Princess, "Counselor, I wish to speak to you. I do not know you. Come closer so I may see your face."

The Princess was startled and replied, without thinking, "Oh, Father, I cannot." When she realized her slip, she felt exposed and covered her face.

The King roared, "Who is this who calls me 'Father'? Why are you hiding your face? Show yourself."

The Princess turned her face and dropped her hand and hood so that her Father could gaze upon her. "Is this my daughter? What am I to do with such boldness? Leave me!"

The Princess fled to the garden where she sat rocking and trembling.

The King paced and pondered and at last went to the garden. He took his daughter's hands and said, "My daughter, my dove. I want to open my heart and mind to you. Will you come and sit at my right hand? Will you be my mercy?"

"Yes, my lord and gracious King," replied the Princess. "I will."

Through the long years ahead, the kingdom was ruled with more kindness than justice required.

8 **mentor:** a trusted counselor; guide

9 **temper:** soften; tone down

10 **litigants:** those involved in a lawsuit or legal dispute

Portia's Speech

FROM *THE MERCHANT OF VENICE*

WILLIAM SHAKESPEARE

The quality of mercy is not strain'd.
It droppeth as the gentle rain from heaven
Upon the place beneath. It is twice bless'd:
It blesseth him that gives and him that takes.
'Tis mightiest in the mightiest; it becomes
The throned monarch better than his crown.
His scepter shows the force of temporal power;
The attribute to awe and majesty,
Wherein doth sit the dread and fear of kings;
But mercy is above this scepted sway;
It is enthroned in the hearts of kings;
It is an attribute to God himself,
And earthly power doth then show likest God's
When mercy seasons justice.

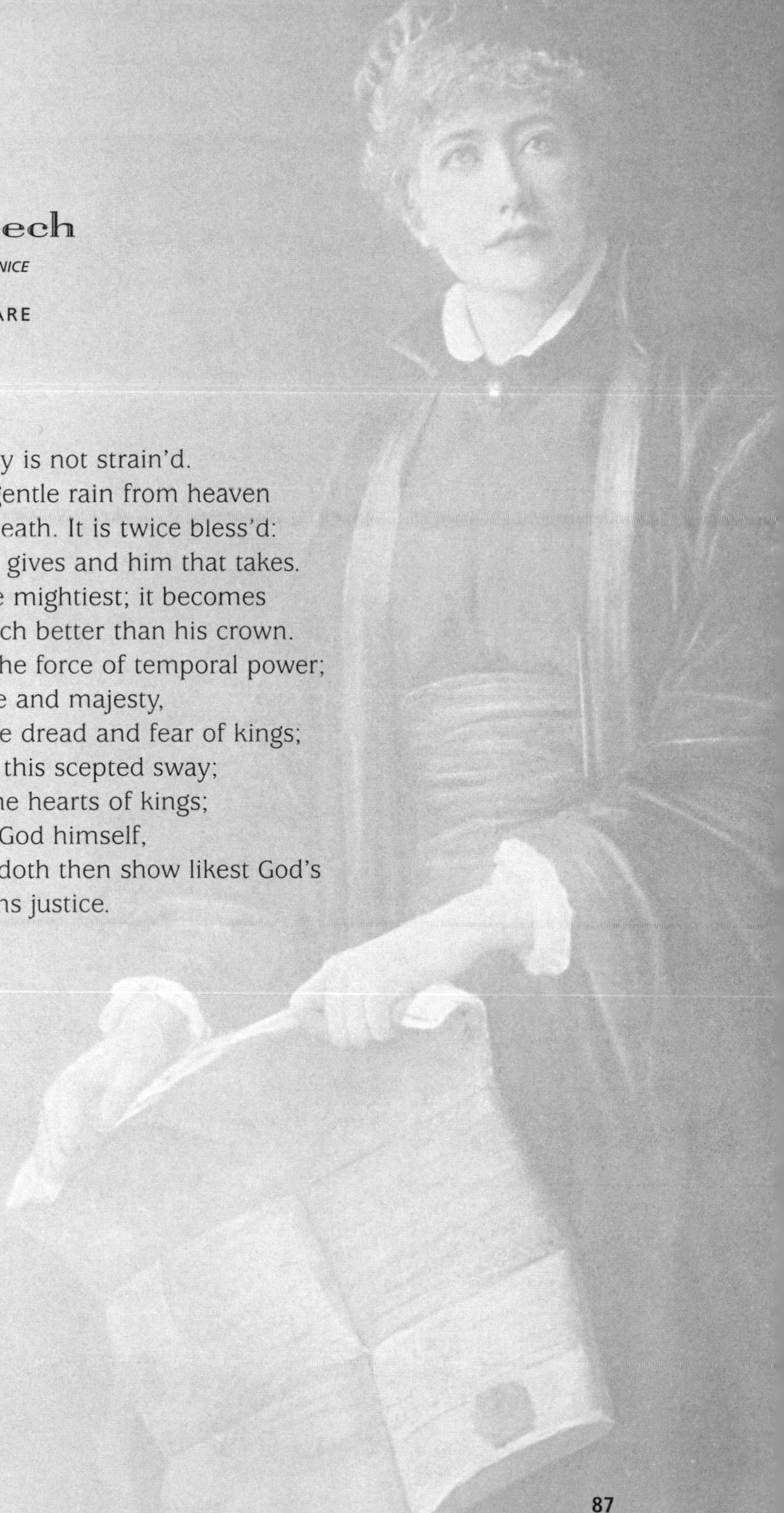

ELLEN TERRY AS PORTIA
Louise Jopling

The Bishop's Candlesticks

Lewy Olfson
Based on Victor Hugo's *Les Misérables*

CHARACTERS

Jean Valjean

Voice of the judge

Mademoiselle Fleury

Madame Magloire

Bishop

Three gendarmes

STUDY FOR A MALE FIGURE FOR *BURIAL IN CAMPINE*
1888
Theodor Verstraete

PROLOGUE

Before the curtains. The stage is dark, except for a spotlight on JEAN VALJEAN, *who stands abjectly to one side, his hands tied behind his back, his head bowed. He is a middle-aged man, very poorly dressed. The* VOICE OF THE JUDGE *is heard, loud and sonorous, over a loudspeaker system.* VALJEAN *does not react to what he hears, except, perhaps, that he seems to become more and more abject. (Note: If desired, the* JUDGE *may be played by an actor who appears at the other side of the stage.)*

VOICE OF THE JUDGE. Jean Valjean, for the attempted theft of a loaf of bread, you are sentenced to five years at hard labor. *(The sound of a gavel rapped three times is heard.)*

Jean Valjean, for escaping from the galleys after four years of serving your sentence, your time is hereby extended an additional three years. *(The gavel is rapped three times.)*

Jean Valjean, for attempted escape during your sixth year of imprisonment, and for resisting capture, your sentence is extended five years—two with the double chain. *(The gavel is rapped three times.)*

Jean Valjean, for attempted escape and for four hours of freedom, your time shall be extended three years. *(The gavel is rapped three times again. There is a pause.)*

Jean Valjean, you have spent nineteen years in prison. You have served your sentence. *(Pause)* Jean Valjean, you are free. *(For the first time,* VALJEAN *raises his head. His expression is blank.)*

Editor's Note

French titles are used throughout this play.

Mademoiselle (MLLE.): title for unmarried woman
Madame (MME.): title for married woman
Monseigneur: title for a male dignitary
Monsieur: title of respect for any adult male

VALJEAN *(without emotion).* I have served nineteen years in prison, for stealing a loaf of bread. And now . . . I am free. *(The spotlight goes out, and the curtain opens immediately.)*

SCENE 1

TIME: *About eight o'clock in the evening. Fall, 1815.*
SETTING: *The front room of the Bishop's home.*

AT RISE: MADAME MAGLOIRE, *a middle-aged portly housekeeper, and her friend,* MADEMOISELLE FLEURY, *a spinster of the same age, are sitting over their teacups, gossiping.*

MLLE. FLEURY (*surprised*). You mean to say you haven't heard about him?

MME. MAGLOIRE. No, I must confess I have not.

MLLE. FLEURY. But, my dear, the whole town is talking about him. The ugliest man I have ever seen, I assure you.

MME. MAGLOIRE. I thought you said that nobody has seen him.

MLLE. FLEURY. Nobody has seen him for the last three days, my dear. But before that, he made application for a room at the inn, and they had a good look at him there. They turned him away, of course.

MME. MAGLOIRE. Of course. But then, you have not seen the man himself?

MLLE. FLEURY. Well, no, not personally. But the innkeeper's wife got a good look at him in the candlelight, and she told the laundress all about it. Now, you know how laundresses love to talk, so naturally my laundress got a complete description. Of course, I would never gossip with a common laundress, but fortunately she told the cook all about it. Well, when the cook came running to Mamma with the story—what could Mamma do but listen? And then, of course, Mamma told me. So I can tell you for a fact that this vagabond is the ugliest man in the world. Everyone is talking about him. They say he's probably a runaway convict, but I say he's more likely a murderer at the very least.

MME. MAGLOIRE. Lord in Heaven, it's a wonder we aren't all killed in our beds.

MLLE. FLEURY. It is indeed, Madame Magloire, considering how useless the police are in this town.

MME. MAGLOIRE. But surely the constable[1] has been alerted to the fact that there's a desperate criminal running about.

MLLE. FLEURY (*airily*). Oh, I have no doubt he's been alerted, for all the good it will do. You know what ill will there is between the prefect[2] and the mayor. They're more concerned with doing each other harm than they are with doing any of the rest of us good. So it's little protection we can expect from the police. No, no, we must all become our own police, and guard ourselves as best we can.

MME. MAGLOIRE. You're lucky, Mademoiselle Fleury, that at least you have your brother living with you. That must be some comfort, I'm sure.

MLLE. FLEURY. It is, of course. But then you have the Bishop.

MME. MAGLOIRE. It's little protection I'd get from him, I'm afraid. He's strong enough, Heaven knows, and not wanting in courage. But he's so intent on considering the goodness in man that he never will give a thought to man's wickedness. Not that I mean to speak against God's work, but it does seem to me that our good Bishop is much too trusting.

MLLE. FLEURY (*rising and preparing to go*). If I were you, my dear, I'd just lock the bolts tight when I go to bed . . . and then be extra careful in my prayers.

MME. MAGLOIRE (*laughing ironically*). Lock the bolts! That's a good one. I've been after the Bishop for years to put a decent lock on the doors, but he won't hear of it. (*An offstage clock begins to chime eight.*)

MLLE. FLEURY. Eight o'clock already. Really, I must be going. I don't want that murderer to attack me on my way through the square.

MME. MAGLOIRE. And I must begin setting the table for dinner. One thing I can say for the Bishop—he is always punctual.

MLLE. FLEURY. Well, I wish I could stay and wish him a good evening, but with all these murderers and vagabonds and scoundrels about, one can't be too careful.

(BISHOP *enters. He is a wise, strong-willed but gentle man in his mid-fifties.*)

1 **constable:** public official responsible for keeping the peace

2 **prefect:** a chief officer or local judge

(BISHOP *enters. He is a wise, strong-willed but gentle man in his mid-fifties.*)

MME. MAGLOIRE. Ah, Monseigneur, Mademoiselle Fleury was just regretting that she had to leave before you came. But you are just in time.

BISHOP. Good evening, Mademoiselle Fleury. I hope you are well.

MLLE. FLEURY. As well as can be expected, thank you, Monseigneur. I do apologize for dashing off like this, but with all that's going on in the town these days, I really don't like to be out too late. And it gets dark so early at this time of year; have you noticed that?

BISHOP (*dryly*). I believe it happens regularly in that fashion every year at this season.

MLLE. FLEURY (*vaguely*). Yes, I suppose it does. Well, good night to you.

BISHOP. Good night, Mademoiselle. I hope you may reach home safely.

MME. MAGLOIRE. It was so nice talking to you, my dear. Do come again.

MLLE. FLEURY. I will, thank you. Goodbye. (*She goes out.* MME. MAGLOIRE *begins to set the table.* BISHOP *sits down.*)

MME. MAGLOIRE (*as she works*). Poor Mademoiselle Fleury. I should not wish to be in her shoes right now, walking across the square unescorted. (*Not getting any response, she tries again.*) I suppose you've heard the talk in town, Monseigneur.

BISHOP (*calmly*). I heard something of it indistinctly. Are we in any great danger, then?

MME. MAGLOIRE (*happy to be able to continue her gossip*). I should say we are, Monseigneur. There's a mysterious vagabond hiding about.

BISHOP (*without curiosity*). Oh?

MME. MAGLOIRE. A terribly ugly man, with a rope, they say, and a cloth sack. Nobody knows quite who he is, but everybody is agreed that something will happen tonight. The police are so badly organized. To live in this mountainous country, and not even have street lights—it is too barbaric. You know, Monseigneur, we really ought to get some bolts and other proper fastenings for the door.

BISHOP. A latch is quite sufficient, Madame Magloire. A bishop's door should be ever ready to open.

MME. MAGLOIRE. But with this runaway in town, this murderer! This house is not safe at all—even if you are the Bishop. And if you will permit me, I should like to go to the blacksmith shop tomorrow and get some bolts. For I say that a door which opens by a latch on the outside to the first comer, why, nothing could be more horrible. And then, you have the habit of saying "Come in" even at midnight, no matter who it is that may knock. As though there were even need to knock. One might just raise the latch . . . (*There is a knock at the door.*)

BISHOP (*who has not been listening too closely*). Come in.

MME. MAGLOIRE. There, you see? You just say "Come in" as though there were no harm in the world . . . (JEAN VALJEAN *enters, carrying a cloth sack.* MME. MAGLOIRE shrieks.) Good heavens! It's he!

BISHOP (*gently, to* VALJEAN). Good evening, my friend. What can I do for you?

VALJEAN (*defiantly, almost angrily*). See here: I will tell you right off who I am. My name is Jean Valjean. I am a convict. I have been nineteen years in the galleys. A week ago I was set free and started for Pontarlier, which is my destination. For four days I walked from Toulon. When I reached this town three days ago, I went to an inn, and they sent me away because of my yellow passport. I went to another inn; they said "Get out." It was the same with one as with another. For two nights I went into the fields to sleep beneath the stars, but there were no stars. A good woman saw me and showed me your house. "Knock there," she said. I have knocked. What is this place? Is it an inn? I have money—my savings, one hundred and nine francs and fifteen sous[3] which I have earned in the galleys by my work for nineteen years. I will pay. What do I care? I have money. I am very tired—and I am so hungry. May I stay?

BISHOP. Madame Magloire, put on another plate.

VALJEAN. Did you understand me? I am a galley-slave—a convict. There is my passport, yellow as you can see. That is enough to have me thrown out wherever I go. Will you read it?

BISHOP (*waving aside the passport*). I do not wish to see it. You may stay here. Sit down and warm yourself, monsieur. We will take supper presently, and your bed will be made while you sup.

3 **francs and sous:** French units of money

MME. MAGLOIRE. But don't you realize who—

BISHOP. Kindly put on an extra plate, as I asked before. (MME. MAGLOIRE *goes to cupboard.*)

VALJEAN (*astonished*). True? True? You will keep me? You will allow me to stay? A convict? You call me "monsieur" and don't say "Get out, dog!" as everybody else does. I thought that you would send me away, so I told you straight off who I am. I shall have a supper and a bed, like other people, with a mattress, and sheets?

BISHOP. Of course you shall, my good man.

VALJEAN. It is nineteen years since I have slept in a bed . . .

MME. MAGLOIRE (*peremptorily*). If I may offer my opinion . . .

BISHOP (*interrupting her gently, but looking at her sternly*). Madame Magloire, as we have a guest for dinner, we must use the good silver. Will you fetch it? (*Upset and angry,* MME. MAGLOIRE *goes to cupboard and takes down the silver, muttering to herself.*)

VALJEAN. Tell me, monsieur, who are you who treats me so kindly? You are an innkeeper, aren't you? I will pay you well.

BISHOP. I am a priest who lives here, monsieur.

VALJEAN (*happily*). Oh, Monsieur le Curé, every time you call me "monsieur," it is like water to a dying man.

BISHOP. After dinner is prepared, Madame Magloire, you must make ready the room next to mine for our guest. You will feel much better after a good night's rest, eh, monsieur?

VALJEAN (*curiously*). You are going to let me sleep in the room next to your own? Have you reflected upon it? Who tells you that I am not a murderer?

BISHOP (*simply*). God will take care of that. Madame Magloire, the light grows dim. Should we not have some candlelight?

MME. MAGLOIRE (*sullenly*). Ah, I understand. You wish me to use the silver candlesticks as well as the silver plates (*contemptuously*) for our guest.

VALJEAN. Monsieur le Curé, you are good. You don't despise me. (MME. MAGLOIRE *goes to the mantelpiece and takes down two heavy silver* *candlesticks. She puts them on the table.* VALJEAN *continues speaking.*) You take me into your house. You give me supper; you will light your candles for me. And I haven't hidden from you where I come from and how miserable I am.

BISHOP. You need not tell me who you are. This is not my house. It is the house of God. It does not ask any comer whether he has a name, but whether he has an affliction. You are suffering; you are hungry and thirsty; be welcome. And do not thank me. Do not tell me that I take you into my house. This is the home of no man, except him who needs asylum.[4] I tell you, who are a traveler, that you are more at home here than I. Whatever is here is yours.

VALJEAN (*overwhelmed, and on the point of tears*). Stop, stop, Monsieur le Curé. You are so kind that I don't know what I am. All that is gone.

BISHOP. Shall I tell you what you are? I had no need to ask your name. I knew you before you told me.

VALJEAN (*astonished*). Really? You knew me?

BISHOP (*simply*). Yes. Stranger, you are my brother. (Bishop *quietly sits at the table.* VALJEAN *stares at him in wonder.* MME. MAGLOIRE *throws up her hands and sighs, as the curtain falls.*)

▲ ▲ ▲

SCENE 2

TIME: *Early the next morning.*
SETTING: *The same.*

AT RISE: *The stage is lighted dimly through the window. A clock chimes five. After a moment,* JEAN VALJEAN *comes into the room. He moves stealthily and quietly. He pauses in the center for a moment, shakes his head and puts his hand to his forehead. He goes to the window, opens it, looks out. Then he*

4 **asylum:** a place of refuge and protection

goes to the cupboard, opens it softly and takes out silver basket. Occasionally looking about to make sure he is not being watched, he puts the silver, piece by piece, into the crude sack he carries. When he has loaded the sack, he tosses empty basket out of the window, gives one last look around the room, and then stealthily climbs out through the window. This pantomime is not rushed, but there is a feeling of sustained suspense. The lights black out to denote the passage of a few hours. After a pause, the clock chimes seven. The lights come up and fill the room. It is day. MME. MAGLOIRE *is setting the table for breakfast. After a moment, the* BISHOP *enters, carrying the empty silver basket, which he casually sets on a chair by the door.*

MME. MAGLOIRE. Back from your morning walk, Monseigneur?

BISHOP. It is a glorious morning, Madame Magloire. It did me good to stroll around the garden. *(Laughing slightly)* Our guest has not stirred himself yet?

MME. MAGLOIRE. I haven't heard a sound out of him this morning.

BISHOP. Poor man, he must be exhausted. Well, it will do him good to sleep late.

MME. MAGLOIRE. I'll set the table for three for breakfast. I'll wager he'll be up fast enough when he smells the bacon frying. *(She goes to the cupboard and begins taking out plates, etc.)*

BISHOP. You're probably right. He had a hearty enough appetite for his dinner last night, but it will be several days before he feels he has had all the food he wants.

MME. MAGLOIRE *(at the cupboard; to herself)*. That's strange—I was sure I had put it back in here.

BISHOP. What's that, Madame Magloire?

MME. MAGLOIRE. The silver basket. I was certain I put it back into the cupboard last night. And now it isn't there.

BISHOP. If it is the silver basket you are looking for, it is over there on the chair.

MME. MAGLOIRE *(going to it, relieved)*. Heaven be praised! I didn't know what had become of—but—but there is nothing in it! Where is the silver?

BISHOP. Ah, it is the silver, then, that troubles you. I do not know where that is.

MME. MAGLOIRE *(shrieks).* Good Heavens, it is stolen! That man who came last night must have stolen it!

BISHOP *(protesting).* Now, Madame Magloire . . .

MME. MAGLOIRE *(angrily).* We'll see soon enough if I am right. *(She dashes off to investigate the bedrooms.)*

BISHOP *(looking after her, a slight frown on his face).* Let us hope you are wrong. *(More softly)* But, of course, if you are right, it would explain how the silver basket came to be lying in the garden. And how the window came to be open. (MME. MAGLOIRE *returns.)*

MME. MAGLOIRE. It is just as I suspected, Monseigneur. The man has gone and the silver is stolen. *(She runs to the window.)* See, here is how he got out—through the window, so he would not be seen. I warned you to mend that hole in the garden wall where anyone might enter, but you would never listen. Now this is the price we have to pay for your foolishness. That abominable fellow has gone, and stolen our silver!

BISHOP *(mildly).* You must calm yourself, Madame Magloire. In the first place, did this silver belong to us? Consider. I have for a long time wrongfully withheld this silver. It belonged to the poor. Who was this man? A poor man, evidently.

MME. MAGLOIRE. Alas, it is not for my sake that I am so upset. It's all the same to me. But it is on your account, Monseigneur. What are you going to eat from now?

BISHOP *(surprised).* How so? Have we not tin plates?

MME. MAGLOIRE. But tin smells.

BISHOP. Well, then, we can eat from iron plates, I suppose.

MME. MAGLOIRE. Iron tastes bad.

BISHOP. Wooden plates, then. It is all one to me.

MME. MAGLOIRE *(horrified).* Was there ever such an idea? The Bishop decides to eat from wooden plates! Monsiegneur, it is not proper. Oh, when I think of it! To take a man in like that, and to give him food and a bed. And then to have the silver stolen from us in the night. But, I must say it's a mercy he did nothing but steal. We might have been murdered in our beds. Oh, I tried to warn you, Monseigneur.

Mademoiselle Fleury and I, we both tried to warn you.

BISHOP *(beginning to lose his temper).* Really, Madame Magloire, you begin to put me out of patience. The next thing I know you will have yourself convinced that the poor man did indeed kill us, and that masses ought to be sung for the repose of our souls.

MME. MAGLOIRE *(offended).* You may treat the matter lightly if you like, Monseigneur. But as for me—the very thought of it makes chills run all over me. We could have been killed!

BISHOP. For the last time, may I remind you that we were *not* killed? *(There is a knock at the door.)* Come in, come in. *(Three* GENDARMES[5] *enter, dragging* VALJEAN *along with them. The* 1ST GENDARME *carries the sack of silver. The* 2ND GENDARME *holds a rope tied around* VALJEAN*'s wrists behind his back.* VALJEAN *hangs his head; he has become, once again, abject as earlier.)*

MME. MAGLOIRE *(in amazement).* It's he! They've taken him prisoner!

1ST GENDARME. Excuse us for bothering you, Monseigneur . . .

VALJEAN *(looking up, surprised).* Monseigneur? Then you are not the curé?[6]

2ND GENDARME *(roughly, to* VALJEAN*).* Silence! It is Monseigneur, the Bishop.

BISHOP *(to* VALJEAN, *jovially).* Good morning, Monsieur Valjean. I am glad to see you again. Forgive me for not having been awake when you left this morning.

MME. MAGLOIRE. Monseigneur, what do you—?

3RD GENDARME. Then you know this man, Monseigneur?

BISHOP *(smoothly).* Of course I know him.

MME. MAGLOIRE *(angrily).* Monseigneur . . .

BISHOP *(interrupting).* But tell me, Monsieur Valjean, why did you not take the candlesticks as well?

VALJEAN *(confused).* The—the candlesticks?

BISHOP. Don't you remember?

5 **gendarmes:** armed French police officers

6 **curé:** parish priest

OPEN BIBLE, EXTINGUISHED CANDLE, AND NOVEL
1885
Vincent Van Gogh

VALJEAN *(in a daze).* Remember? No, nothing.

BISHOP. When I gave you the silver, I also gave you the candlesticks. They are silver, too. They would bring a good price—at least two hundred francs, if not more. Why did you not take them along with your plates? Fetch the candlesticks, Madame Magloire.

MME. MAGLOIRE *(angrily doing as he tells her).* Don't tell me there is any silver left in the house!

BISHOP *(calmly).* They are on the mantelpiece, Madame Magloire, where they are always kept.

1ST GENDARME. Then what this man said was true, Monseigneur? We met him in the square. He seemed to be running away, so we arrested him to ask him a few questions. We found this—his sack full of silver.

BISHOP *(interrupting with a smile).* And he told you that it had been given to him by a good old priest with whom he had passed the night. I see it all.

2ND GENDARME. That is *exactly* what he told us.

BISHOP. So you brought him back here to see if he was telling the truth . . . or, more precisely, because you were sure he was *not* telling the truth. It is all a mistake.

1ST GENDARME. Our apologies. If that is so, we can let him go.

MME. MAGLOIRE *(furious).* You're going to let them—?

BISHOP *(ignoring her).* By all means, let him go. The poor man is innocent of any wrongdoing.

1ST GENDARME *(abruptly to the other* GENDARMES). Untie him. We have made a mistake.

VALJEAN. Is it . . . is it true that they are letting me go?

2ND GENDARME *(rudely).* Did you not hear the Bishop? You are free.

VALJEAN *(muttering to himself, as he is being untied).* Free . . . free.

BISHOP *(to the* GENDARMES). Gentlemen, I thank you for your trouble.

3RD GENDARME. Our apologies, Monseigneur. We did not know this man was your friend. We were only doing our duty.

BISHOP. Of course, of course. I understand. Good morning to you.

2ND GENDARME. Thank you, Monseigneur. Sorry to have made a mistake. Good morning. *(The* GENDARMES *exit, looking puzzled. When the door is closed, the* BISHOP *turns to* MME. MAGLOIRE *with a slightly ironic smile.)*

BISHOP. And you were complaining, Madame Magloire, about the inadequacy of the police in this town.

VALJEAN *(unable to believe what has happened).* And I—I am really free to go?

BISHOP. Of course, my friend. But before you go, here are your candlesticks. Take them.

VALJEAN *(trembling as he takes them).* Why? Why do you do this for me?

BISHOP. I have told you. You are my brother. By the way, my friend, when you come again, you need not come through the garden. You can always come in and go out by the front door. It is closed only with a latch, day and night.

VALJEAN *(confused).* You—you would let me return? After all that has happened? I must be dreaming. Everything is spinning around in my head. I am so confused.

BISHOP. Go in peace, my friend. But never forget that you have promised me to use this silver to become an honest man.

VALJEAN. But I—I do not remember. I do not recollect your giving me the silver, or my giving you a promise. I remember . . .

BISHOP *(urgently).* Forget what you remember! Your memories of the past are all a dream now. I give you the silver freely. And I want your solemn promise that you will use it to become an honest man. Promise me that you will start a new way of life. A new life!

VALJEAN *(considering).* An honest man. *(Happily)* Yes, yes. I *will* start a new life. I promise!

BISHOP. Jean Valjean . . . my brother. You no longer belong to evil, but to good. It is your soul that I am buying for you. I withdraw it from dark thoughts and from the spirit of perdition forever, and I give it to God. *(*VALJEAN *kneels at the* BISHOP*'s feet. The* BISHOP *places his hand on* VALJEAN*'s head and looks upwards.* MME. MAGLOIRE *looks on, touched and thoughtful, as the curtain falls.)*

The End

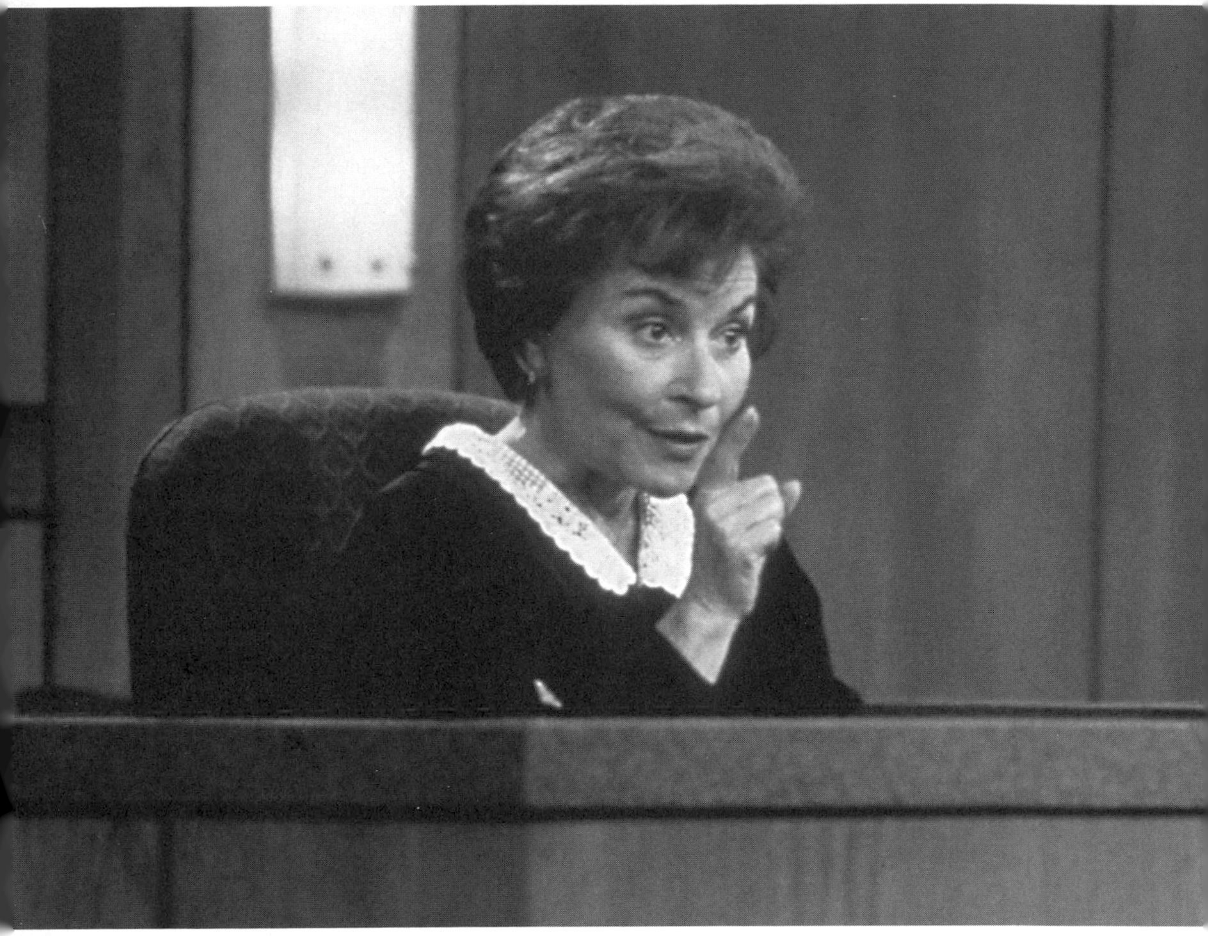

Judge Judy Sheindlin

This Isn't Kiddy Court

Judge Judy Sheindlin

Judge Judy Sheindlin has been a New York City prosecutor of juvenile offenders and a family court judge. After being featured on "60 Minutes" as a tough judge, a television producer hired her to star in her own show in 1996.

When my son Adam was six years old, we lived in a typical suburban home. I was an attorney practicing in Manhattan Family Court. Adam was a beautiful but very precocious child, always looking for an angle or advantage. I used to think that when he grew up, I would be visiting him either at his palatial estate or once a month in some prison upstate.

After a long day of prosecuting delinquents, I pulled into my driveway to find Adam sitting with a box of caps and banging them with a rock to make them explode. Under my rigorous and relentless cross-examination, he finally confessed that he had ridden his bike to the corner store and stolen the caps. This was the test of my parenting; this could be his turning point.

I quickly put Adam in the car and drove to the store, where he sheepishly apologized for the theft. I told the storekeeper that if he ever saw him in the store alone again, to call the police and arrest him. Today, Adam is an assistant district attorney in New York and that story seems very, very old.

Or is it?

When I first confronted Adam with what he had done, he treated it as a game. Just like thousands of other kids who parade through our criminal justice system today. Juvenile violence is skyrocketing across the nation and adults are largely to blame. I cannot tell you how many times I have seen delinquents walk out of our courtrooms, laughing at victims and at the non-punishments they receive. Laughing at the judge and laughing at the system.

The numbers are not funny: In 1979, there were an estimated 70,000 kids in juvenile institutions nationwide. In 1991. . . the number rose to more than 90,000. In 1994, the Criminal Justice Institute estimated that 100,000 or more kids were in custody, in adult as well as juvenile facilities. In cities, suburbs and rural communities we see the same stories on television every night about youngsters breaking the law and winding up behind bars. We hear the same heart-wrenching stories from victims, the same cries of parents, educators and law enforcement officials: Where have we gone wrong, and how can we fix it?

Let's start with common sense. By failing to set strict limits for children—in the home, in the school and in society as a whole—we aggravate the very problems we're trying to solve. By winking at abuse, covering up criminal behavior or explaining it away, we have created a monstrous dilemma for law enforcement.

Most of us know that foster care programs nationwide have been a disaster, and by 1998, many of these kids will turn thirteen. As the products of dysfunctional homes, too many of them will undoubtedly enter our juvenile justice system. This might be our last chance to do something about their future, and our own safety. Here are a few suggestions:

1. Hard time is good. Good time is a joke.

Convicted juveniles, like adult offenders, often gain early and undeserved release from jail. In my opinion, good time should be earned for productivity; it should not be a reward that accumulates just by stepping inside prison walls. Juveniles should qualify for early release only if they complete a course of academic or vocational studies. Let us reward those who do the right thing, but keep those who are not motivated behind bars for their full term.

Once, when I sat in Bronx Family Court in 1985, I reviewed the case of a fifteen-year-old boy who had three convictions to his credit, two of them violent. I was amazed when the case was called and he was led into court not only in handcuffs, but in leg irons as well. He stood about six foot three and must have weighed 280 pounds. The boy stood there with his mother, his attorney, the prosecutor and a representative of the state institution where he had been confined.

I read the file carefully and learned that this young man had been in four different facilities, none of which were able to contain his violent behavior. While the state had originally asked that he be confined for an additional twelve months, it had now changed its mind and wanted to release him. Why? I asked. The state's answer was simple and chilling. "We have done all we can for him, Your Honor, and he has exhausted our service," said the representative. I was dumbstruck. He had not only exhausted their services, but clearly had sapped their sanity. Then the young man's mother interrupted, saying, "I don't know what you're going to do with him if you let him go. But he ain't coming home with me!" I did what I believed was the only sane thing, and put him back in custody for another year. Maybe they could not help him, but at least we would know where he was. The idea that he would be out roaming the streets was unthinkable.

2. REWARD THE PRODUCTIVE, NOT THE UNPRODUCTIVE.

Taxpayers made it clear in the last election that they were no longer willing to support costly programs that have a long history of failure. Rehabilitation is a laudable goal, but when you spend millions and do not even come close to reaching that goal, it is time for a new broom. We have a special legacy[1] of failure when it comes to changing the lives of youthful offenders, and still the dollars—and the bodies of victims—pile up.

The fact is, we have been focusing on a small minority of the kids who come from poor, dysfunctional homes. The vast majority of these children suffer from neglected schools and streets, and yet do not commit crimes. Most kids struggle within these chaotic environments, with little or no support, and yet try to do the right thing. But we have ignored them. For years, our social and fiscal[2] emphasis has been on those few who break the law. We leave the good kids to fend for themselves.

A recent set of photographs in my local newspaper illustrated this crazy inversion[3] of priorities. In one picture was a state-of-the-art gymnasium, with Nautilus equipment and gleaming free weights. It was part of the recreational complex at an upstate detention facility. The other photo was an overcrowded, deteriorated inner city junior high school. The paint peeling off the walls and broken windows were symbols of how little we value our law-abiding children.

1 **legacy:** something handed down
2 **fiscal:** related to financial matters
3 **inversion:** reversal

What kind of insanity is this? We should scale down our juvenile justice facilities and adult prisons to the bare minimum, offering offenders food, clothes and a bed, vocational and academic training. Period. Meanwhile, we should take the money we save from "dressing up" our detention facilities and spend it on the good kids who are struggling just to get by. We should let them know that we are doing this to invest in them and their communities, to show that we appreciate their struggle and want them to succeed. We should offer them part-time or after-school jobs. If society does not acknowledge their importance to our future, many more will fall prey to the mean streets.

3. For kids who have a chance, group homes are the answer.

Sometimes, juveniles need more than a program to change their lives. A loving environment can work wonders. Many kids have to be removed from their communities, not because of the ferocity of their crimes, but because they come from dysfunctional homes. From what I have seen, no interventions will fix these parents—certainly not while their children are still children.

Consider the case of George, a fifteen-year-old boy who appeared in family court on his first offense. It was a nonviolent crime and did not appear to be serious. He accepted full responsibility for what he had done, and when I read the probation report describing his history and home life, my jaw dropped.

He had skipped school far more often than he attended, but the reason was heart-wrenching: His father was an abusive alcoholic who regularly beat his mother in their home. George knew that his father became particularly destructive after a drinking binge so he stayed home to protect his mother. She was unwilling to file charges, and George had become the family protector. Here was a young man who, through no fault of his own, had been entirely deprived of childhood. Now, he faced the prospect of being institutionalized. To keep him at home meant we would lose any chance to improve his life. He was doomed to become a dysfunctional, uneducated adult.

What we need for kids like George are small group homes. He was not a predator, he was a gentle and basically moral kid. What he required was a healthy environment. Given the state of our economy, many houses these days are cheap. If the state purchased a $250,000 home to shelter four such kids—who lived there with in-house parents—these youngsters might have a decent shot. Obviously, we would screen these caretakers carefully. We would want them to have an education and parenting skills. But think of the numbers: In one year, you would pay for the cost of the house, considering the $75,000 tab to house an individual kid in a state facility. Even if you paid an additional $5,000 per year for food, clothing and incidentals, you would be saving four lives—and a lot of money.

4. Let us put reality back into the system—starting with language.

The legislatures of each state should send a clear message that the priority of the juvenile justice system is protecting the citizenry. They could begin by improving their English.

In most states, the trial of a delinquency case has all the safeguards of an adult trial. Yet we muddy up the proceedings with a legal gibberish that does not say what it means. It is confusing to everyone—to police, judges, juveniles and, most of all, the public. In New York, for example, a juvenile is not accused of a crime. He is accused of "an act which, if committed by an adult, would be a crime." A juvenile is not called a defendant, but a respondent. A prosecutor is not called a prosecutor, but a petitioner. A trial is called a fact-finding hearing. A sentencing is a dispositional hearing. And a conviction is not a conviction; it is a finding. Can we get some reality in here? If some punk bashes your head with a baseball bat, we should not call this an "incident." We should call it what it is—a crime, a felony. Soupy language is stupid and diminishes the justice system.

We should also eliminate the rules of confidentiality affecting juveniles. Legislators fail to protect the public when they make it impossible for judges to know a young offender's full criminal history at the time of sentencing. They only protect a misguided sense of fairness. We have to abandon old arguments that we are stigmatizing[4] youngsters by making their criminal records available for inspection, or by fingerprinting and photographing them. This is old-fashioned pandering,[5] and juvenile crime stopped being old-fashioned years ago. Citizens have a right to know who is living next door. Do they want a teenage babysitter who also happens to be a convicted drug dealer or sex offender? You cannot make responsible judgements without good information, and that is true whether you are a judge or a neighbor.

4 **stigmatizing:** identifying in a negative manner

5 **pandering:** assisting others to persist in criminal acts

5. We need a national curfew.

Most lawbreaking by youngsters takes place at a time when these kids should be at home. If they were reasonably supervised by parents, this would not be a problem. But they are not, and since juvenile crime is skyrocketing, we need stronger protections. I recommend imposing a national curfew for kids under eighteen, and believe me, that is not as harsh as it sounds. When I was growing up, my parents set a curfew for me. On school nights it was nine P.M. and on weekends it was midnight. Maybe you had the same experience, or know someone who did. Either way, you learned to live with those rules. If the parents of today's children cannot or will not set similar limits, then society must do it for them, for their protection—and its own.

6. CCC—Career criminal control

Judges should have the option of imposing consecutive sentences on particularly violent juveniles, just as they do on adults. When it comes to kids who rape, maim and kill, their age quickly becomes unimportant.

For those juveniles who become second offenders, there should be the option of a fixed sentence followed by a conditional release until age twenty-five. I call this career criminal control for troublesome kids. The conditions for their release from custody would be simple: No arrests, full-time employment or school, and a weekly check-in with the local police precinct. You would *have* to be registered.

7. End parole and probation—not just for kids, for everyone.

In New York, the recidivism[6] rate for juveniles is 75 percent, and the adult rate is close to that. What this tells me is that probation is not working, just as early release programs from prison—which we call parole—are not working. So let us have the courage to change. I am calling for the total elimination of probation and parole as we know it. In their place, probationers and parolees would be required to register at their local precinct and check in each week with a police officer. This would free up billions, and that money could be used to build more jails, to hire more police, to fight crime more intelligently. In time, the local precinct would come to know all the local lawbreakers, and you can imagine the sobering impact this new policy would have on offenders.

6 **recidivism:** a relapse into previous behavior (in this case, repeated criminal behavior)

Community policing is touted[7] by many liberals as the wave of the future—and this would be the ultimate form of community policing. Let us give it a try. What do we have to lose?

8. No more free lawyers, no more free rides.

Too many people treat the juvenile justice system as a joke, especially the parents of kids who get a taxpayer-supported lawyer and lose little sleep over their children's lawbreaking. That would change overnight if we required them to pay for the attorneys who try to keep their kids out of jail. They should pay according to their means, even if it is a percentage of their welfare benefits. I would make them pay for the cost of incarceration as well. Raising children is a parent's responsibility, and if they have screwed up, taxpayers should not shoulder the entire burden. We have thousands of kids in state institutions, and most of them come from homes on public assistance. In too many states, the welfare keeps flowing while the kids are in jail. This is dumber than dumb. Let us not forget middle-class kids: Their parents claim them as tax deductions—even as the state pays for their upkeep in detention facilities. That, too, must end, and the parents must reimburse the state for housing their failures.

Finally, kids should pay for their crimes. Literally. Many communities have laws which permit judges to order financial restitution from delinquents, but few of them are used. I believe in mandatory juvenile restitution, nationwide. It could be funded from work programs when kids are in custody, or from special projects in the community. If you crack somebody's head open, you should pay a price in more ways than one. We are talking about responsibility: cause and effect, pleasure and pain, right and wrong, order and disorder.

7 **touted:** highly praised

RESPONDING TO CLUSTER THREE

PUNISHMENT OR MERCY?

Thinking Skill COMPARING AND CONTRASTING

1. Using a chart such as the one below, **compare and contrast** the "judges" in the three selections listed. (There may be more than one judge in a selection.) Which would you consider merciful and which seem more punitive? Then choose the judge you feel is the most fair, supporting your selection with examples.

Merciful Judges	Selection	Punitive Judges
	The Quality of Mercy	
	The Bishop's Candlesticks	
	This Isn't Kiddy Court	

2. "The Quality of Mercy" ends with the phrase, "the kingdom was ruled with more kindness than justice required." What could be the strengths and weaknesses of a judge exhibiting "more kindness"?
3. **Irony** refers to the contrast between what is expected and what really happens. In "The Bishop's Candlesticks," what is ironic about Jean Valjean's pardon?
4. **Compare and contrast** the two styles of justice represented by Judge Judy's juvenile courtroom and the peer court format in "And Justice for All" of Cluster Two. Which courtroom would you prefer to be in and why?

Writing Activity: In My Own Words

Write a paraphrase of "Portia's Speech" to make the monologue easier for modern readers.

A Strong Paraphrase

- restates with common usage and syntax
- rewrites the text in a less complex style
- remains true to the original meaning

CLUSTER FOUR

Thinking on Your Own

Thinking Skill SYNTHESIZING

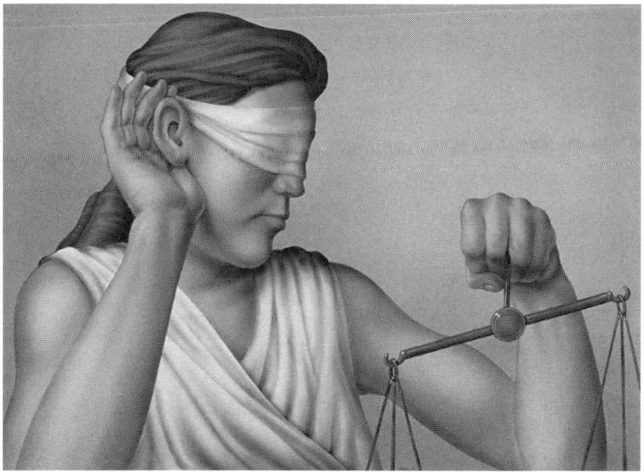

Susan B. Anthony

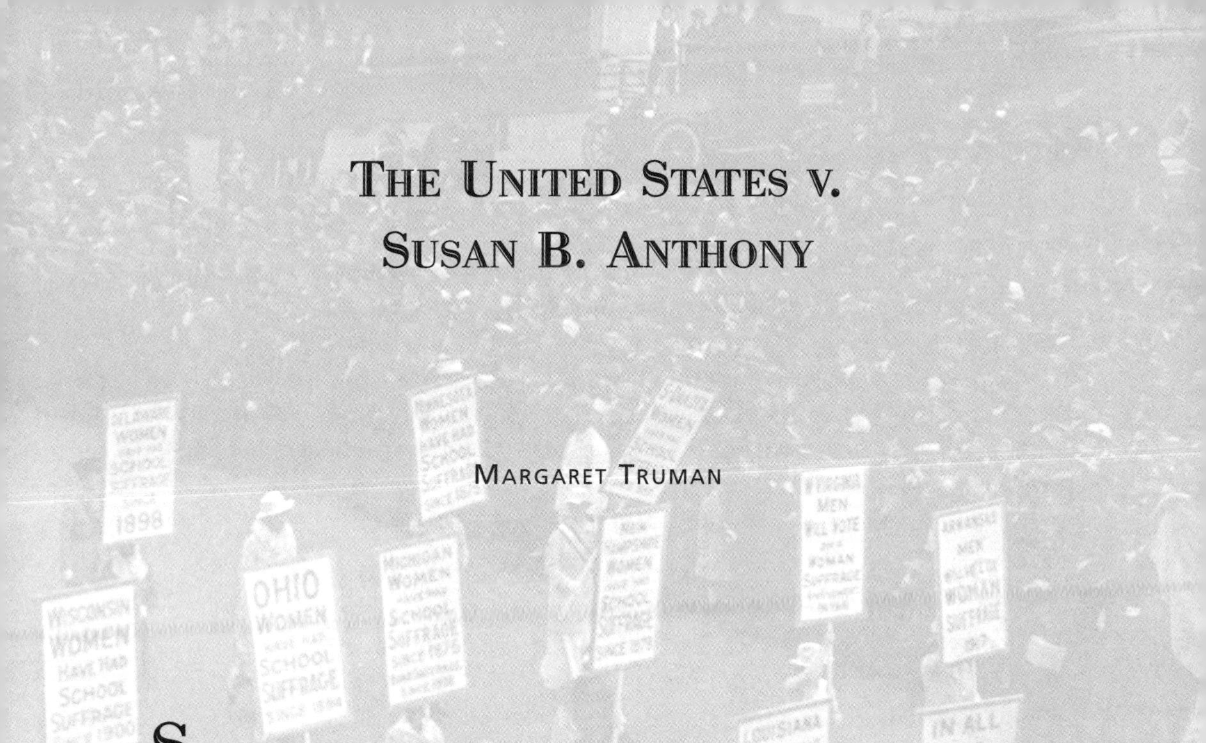

THE UNITED STATES V. SUSAN B. ANTHONY

MARGARET TRUMAN

Susan B. Anthony has never been one of my favorite characters. Stern-eyed and grim-lipped, she seemed utterly devoid of warmth and humor and much too quick to dominate the women she worked with. I always thought her personality could be summed up in one word: battle-ax. On top of that drawback, she was a fanatic. She joined the woman's suffrage movement[1] in 1852, when she was thirty-two years old. From then until her death in 1906, she could think of little else.

The fanatics of one generation have a habit of turning into the heroes and heroines of the next, as Susan B. Anthony proved. And since I've been making a study of heroines, I decided to give Miss Anthony a second look. I have to report that my original assessment of her character was much too harsh. . . .

Susan B. Anthony was a stern and single-minded woman. Like most crusaders for causes—especially unpopular causes—she had little time for fun and games. But I have a sneaky feeling that behind her severe manner and unremitting devotion to duty, she may actually have had a sense of humor. Let me tell you about my favorite episode in Susan B. Anthony's career, and perhaps you'll agree.

It began on Friday morning, November 1, 1872. Susan was reading the morning paper at her home in Rochester. There, at the top of the

1 **woman's suffrage movement:** 19th-century civil rights movement that promoted voting rights for women

editorial page of the *Democrat and Chronicle*, was an exhortation to the city's residents:

> Now register! Today and tomorrow are the only remaining opportunities. If you were not permitted to vote, you would fight for the right, undergo all privations[2] for it, face death for it. You have it now at the cost of five minutes' time to be spent in seeking your place of registration and having your name entered. And yet, on election day, less than a week hence, hundreds of you are likely to lose your votes because you have not thought it worthwhile to give the five minutes. Today and tomorrow are your only opportunities. Register now!

Susan B. Anthony read the editorial again. Just as she thought, it said nothing about being addressed to men only. With a gleam in her eye, she put down the paper and summoned her sister Guelma, with whom she lived. The two women donned their hats and cloaks and went off to call on two other Anthony sisters who lived nearby. Together, the four women headed for the barber shop on West Street, where voters from the Eighth Ward were being registered.

For some time, Susan B. Anthony had been looking for an opportunity to test the Fourteenth Amendment to the Constitution as a weapon to win the vote for women. Adopted in 1868, the amendment had been designed to protect the civil rights—especially the voting rights—of recently freed slaves. It stated that:

> All persons born or naturalized in the United States, and subject to the jurisdiction thereof, are citizens of the United States and of the State wherein they reside. No State shall make or enforce any law which shall abridge the privileges or immunities of citizens of the United States, nor shall any State deprive any person of life, liberty, or property without due process of law, nor deny to any person within its jurisdiction the equal protection of the laws.

▲ ▲ ▲

The amendment did not say that "persons" meant only males, nor did it spell out "the privileges and immunities of citizens." Susan B. Anthony felt perfectly justified in concluding that the right to vote was among the privileges of citizenship and that it extended to women as well as men.

2 **privations:** losses

I'm sure she must have also seen the humor of outwitting the supposedly superior males who wrote the amendment.

It was bad enough for a bunch of women to barge into one sacred male precinct—the barber shop—but to insist on being admitted to another holy of holies—the voting booth—was absolutely outrageous. Mustaches twitched, throats were cleared, a whispered conference was held in the corner.

Susan had brought along a copy of the Fourteenth Amendment. She read it aloud, carefully pointing out to the men in charge of registration that the document failed to state that the privilege of voting extended only to males.

Only one man in the barber shop had the nerve to refuse the Anthony sisters the right to register. The rest buckled under Susan's determined oratory and allowed them to sign the huge, leather-bound voter registration book. If the men in the barber shop thought they were getting rid of a little band of crackpots the easy way, they were wrong. Susan urged all her followers in Rochester to register. The next day, a dozen women invaded the Eighth Ward barber shop, and another thirty-five appeared at registration sites elsewhere in the city. The *Democrat and Chronicle*, which had inadvertently prompted the registrations, expressed no editorial opinion on the phenomenon, but its rival, the *Union and Advertiser*, denounced the women. If they were allowed to vote, the paper declared, the poll inspectors "should be prosecuted to the full extent of the law."

The following Tuesday, November 5, was Election Day. Most of the poll inspectors in Rochester had read the editorial in the *Union and Advertiser* and were too intimidated to allow any of the women who had registered to vote. Only in the Eighth Ward did the males weaken. Maybe the inspectors were *Democrat and Chronicle* readers, or perhaps they were more afraid of Susan B. Anthony than they were of the law. Whatever the reason, when Susan and her sisters showed up at the polls shortly after 7 A.M., there was only a minimum of fuss. A couple of inspectors were hesitant about letting the women vote, but when Susan assured them that she would pay all their legal expenses if they were prosecuted, the men relented, and one by one, the women took their ballots and stepped into the voting booth. There were no insults or sneers, no rude remarks. They marked their ballots, dropped them into the ballot box, and returned to their homes.

Susan B. Anthony's feat quickly became the talk of the country. She was applauded in some circles, vilified in others. But the day of reckoning was not long in arriving. On November 28, Deputy U.S. Marshal E. J. Keeney appeared at her door with a warrant for her arrest. She had violated Section 19 of the Enforcement Act of the Fourteenth Amendment, which held that anyone who voted illegally was to be arrested and tried on criminal charges.

Susan B. Anthony was a great believer in planning ahead. The day after she registered, she decided to get a legal opinion on whether or not she should attempt to vote. A number of lawyers turned her away, but she finally found one who agreed to consider the case. He was Henry R. Selden, a former judge of the Court of Appeals, now a partner in one of Rochester's most prestigious law firms.

▲ ▲ ▲

On the Monday before Election Day, Henry Selden informed his new client that he agreed with her interpretation of the Fourteenth Amendment and that in his opinion, she had every right to cast her ballot. The U.S. Commissioner of Elections in Rochester, William C. Storrs, did not concur.

E. J. Keeney, the marshal dispatched to arrest Susan B. Anthony, was not at all happy with his assignment. He nervously twirled his tall felt hat while waiting for her to come to the front door. When she finally appeared, he blushed and stammered, shifted uncomfortably from one foot to the other, and finally blurted out, "The Commissioner wishes to arrest you."

Susan couldn't help being amused at Keeney's embarrassment. "Is this your usual method of serving a warrant?" she asked calmly. With that, the marshal recovered his official dignity, presented her with the warrant, and told her that he had come to escort her to the office of the Commissioner of Elections.

When Susan asked if she could change into a more suitable dress, the marshal saw his opportunity to escape. "Of course," he said, turning to leave. "Just come down to the Commissioner's office whenever you're ready."

"I'll do no such thing," Susan informed him curtly. "You were sent here to arrest me and take me to court. It's your duty to do so."

Keeney had no choice but to wait while his prisoner went upstairs and put on a more appropriate outfit. When she returned, she thrust out her wrists and said, "Don't you want to handcuff me, too?"

"I assure you, madam," Marshal Keeney stuttered, "it isn't at all necessary."

With the U.S. Marshal at her side, Susan was brought before the Federal Commissioner of Elections, William C. Storrs. Her arrest was recorded, and she was ordered to appear the next day for a hearing. It was conducted by U.S. District Attorney Richard Crowley and his assistant, John E. Pound.

Susan answered District Attorney Crowley's questions politely. She said that she thought the Fourteenth Amendment gave her the right to vote. She admitted that she had consulted an attorney on the question but said that she would have voted even if he had not advised her to do so. When Crowley asked if she had voted deliberately to test the law, she said, "Yes, sir. I have been determined for three years to vote the first time I happened to be at home for the required thirty days before an election."

The District Attorney's next step was to convene a grand jury to draw up a bill of indictment.[3] He and his assistant fell to wrangling over a suitable trial date. Susan interrupted them. "I have lecture dates that will take me to central Ohio," she said. "I won't be available until December 10."

"But you're supposed to be in custody until the hearing," Crowley informed her.

"Is that so?" said Susan coolly. "I didn't know that."

The District Attorney backed down without an argument and scheduled the grand jury session for December 23.

Sixteen women had voted in Rochester. All sixteen were arrested and taken before the grand jury, but Susan alone was brought to trial. The District Attorney had decided to single her out as a test case. The three poll inspectors who had allowed the women to vote were also arrested. The grand jury indicted them too, set bail at five hundred dollars each, and ordered their trial set for the summer term of the U.S. District Court.

Susan Anthony's case now involved nineteen other men and women. All of them—including Susan—were liable to go to prison if they were found guilty and the judge was in a sentencing mood. Prison in the 1870s was a very unpleasant place. There were no minimum security setups where a benevolent government allowed corrupt politicians, crooked labor leaders, and political agitators to rest and rehabilitate, as we do today. Prison meant a cold cell, wretched food, the company of thieves and murderers.

For a while it looked as if Susan might be behind bars even before her trial. She refused to post a bond for her five-hundred-dollar bail. Henry

3 **bill of indictment:** written charge of offense

Selden paid the money for her. "I could not see a lady I respected put in jail," he said.

It must be agonizing to sweat out the weeks before a trial. There is time to look ahead and brood about the possibility of an unfavorable verdict and time to look back, perhaps with regret, at the decision that placed you in the hands of the law. But Susan B. Anthony had no regrets. Nor did she appear to have any anxieties about her trial. She had already proven her fortitude by devoting twenty years of her life to fighting for the right to vote. If she won her case, the struggle would be over. But even if she lost, Susan was not ready to give up the fight. . . .

▲ ▲ ▲

The trial of *The United States* vs. *Susan B. Anthony* opened on the afternoon of June 17, 1873, with the tolling of the Canandaigua Courthouse bell. The presiding justice was Ward Hunt, a prim, pale man, who owed his judgeship to the good offices of Senator Roscoe Conkling, the Republican boss of New York State. Conkling was a fierce foe of woman suffrage, and Hunt, who had no wish to offend his powerful patron, had written his decision before the trial started.

District Attorney Crowley opened the arguments for the prosecution. They didn't make much sense at the time, and in retrospect, they sound nothing short of ridiculous. The District Attorney mentioned that Susan B. Anthony was a woman and therefore she had no right to vote. His principal witness was an inspector of elections for the Eighth Ward, who swore that on November 5 he had seen Miss Anthony put her ballot in the ballot box. To back up his testimony, the inspector produced the voter registration book with Susan B. Anthony's signature in it.

Henry Selden's reply for the defense was equally simple. He contended that Susan Anthony had registered and voted in good faith, believing that it was her constitutional right to do so. When he attempted to call his client to the stand, however, District Attorney Crowley announced that she was not competent to testify in her own behalf. Judge Hunt agreed, and the only thing Henry Selden could do was read excerpts from the testimony Susan had given at her previous hearings when presumably she was no less incompetent than she was right now.

Henry Selden tried to make up for this gross injustice by making his closing argument a dramatic, three-hour speech on behalf of woman suffrage. District Attorney Crowley replied with a two-hour rehash of the original charge.

By the afternoon of June 18, the case of *The United States* vs. *Susan B. Anthony* was ready to go to the jury. It was impossible to predict what their verdict might be, so Judge Hunt, determined to make it the verdict he and Roscoe Conkling wanted, took matters into his own hands. "Gentlemen of the jury," he said, "I direct that you find the defendant guilty."

Henry Selden leaped to his feet. "I object, your honor," he thundered. "The court has no power to direct the jury in a criminal case."

Judge Hunt ignored him. "Take the verdict, Mr. Clerk," he said.

The clerk of the court must have been another Conkling man. "Gentlemen of the jury," he intoned as if the whole proceeding was perfectly normal, "hearken to the verdict as the court hath recorded it. You say you find the defendant guilty of the offense charged. So say you all."

The twelve jurymen looked stunned. They had not even met to discuss the case, much less agree on a verdict. When Henry Selden asked if the clerk could at least poll the jury, Judge Hunt rapped his gavel sharply and declared, "That cannot be allowed. Gentleman of the jury, you are discharged."

An enraged Henry Selden lost no time in introducing a motion for a new trial on the grounds that his client had been denied the right to a jury verdict. Judge Hunt denied the motion. He turned to Susan B. Anthony and said, "The prisoner will stand up. Has the prisoner anything to say why sentence shall not be pronounced?"

Thus far in the trial, Susan B. Anthony had remained silent. Now, she rose to her feet and said slowly, "Yes, your honor, I have many things to say."

▲ ▲ ▲

Without further preliminaries, she launched into a scathing denunciation of Judge Hunt's conduct of her trial. ". . . In your ordered verdict of guilty," she said, "you have trampled underfoot every vital principle of our government. My natural rights, my civil rights, my political rights, are all alike ignored. Robbed of the fundamental privilege of citizenship, I am degraded from the status of a citizen to that of a subject; and not only myself individually, but all of my sex, are, by your honor's verdict, doomed to political subjection under this so-called Republican government."

Judge Hunt reached for his gavel, but Susan B. Anthony refused to be silenced.

"May it please your honor," she continued. "Your denial of my citizen's right to vote is the denial of my right to a trial by a jury of my peers as an offender against law, therefore, the denial of my sacred rights to life, liberty, property, and—"

"The court cannot allow the prisoner to go on," Judge Hunt cried out.

Susan ignored him and continued her impassioned tirade against the court. Hunt frantically rapped his gavel and ordered her to sit down and be quiet. But Susan, who must have been taking delight in his consternation, kept on talking. She deplored the fact that she had been denied the right to a fair trial. Even if she had been given such a trial, she insisted, it would not have been by her peers. Jury, judges, and lawyers were not her equals, but her superiors, because they could vote and she could not. Susan was adamant about the fact that she had been denied the justice guaranteed in the Constitution to every citizen of the United States.

Judge Hunt was sufficiently cowed by now to try to defend himself. "The prisoner has been tried according to the established forms of law," he sputtered.

"Yes, your honor," retorted Susan, overlooking his blatant lie, "but by forms of law all made by men, interpreted by men, administered by men, in favor of men, and against women; and hence your honor's ordered verdict of guilty, against a United States citizen for the exercise of that citizen's right to vote, simply because that citizen was a woman and not a man. But yesterday, the same man-made forms of law declared it a crime punishable with a one-thousand-dollar fine and six months imprisonment for you, or me, or any of us, to give a cup of cold water, a crust of bread, or a night's shelter to a panting fugitive while he was tracking his way to Canada. And every man or woman in whose veins coursed a drop of human sympathy violated that wicked law, reckless of consequences, and was justified in so doing. As, then, the slaves who got their freedom must take it over, or under, or through the unjust forms of law, precisely so now must women, to get their right to a voice in this government, take it, and I have taken mine, and mean to take it at every opportunity."

Judge Hunt flailed his gavel and gave the by now futile order for the prisoner to sit down and be quiet. Susan kept right on talking.

"When I was brought before your honor for trial," she said, "I hoped for a broad and liberal interpretation of the Constitution and its recent amendments. One that would declare all United States citizens under its protection. But failing to get this justice—failing, even, to get a trial by a jury *not* of my peers—I ask not leniency at your hands—but to take the full rigors of the law."

With that Susan finally obeyed Judge Hunt's orders and sat down. Now he had to reverse himself and order her to stand up so he could impose sentence. As soon as he pronounced the sentence—a fine of one hundred dollars plus the costs of prosecuting the trial—Susan spoke up again. "May it please your honor," she said, "I shall never pay a dollar of your unjust penalty. All the stock in trade I possess is a ten-thousand-dollar debt, incurred by publishing my paper—*The Revolution*—four years ago, the sole object of which was to educate all women to do precisely as I have done, rebel against your man-made, unjust, unconstitutional forms of law that tax, fine, imprison, and hang women while they deny them the right of representation in the government; and I shall work on with might and main to pay every dollar of that honest debt, but not a penny shall go to this unjust claim. And I shall earnestly and persistently continue to urge all women to the practical recognition of the old Revolutionary maxim,[4] that 'Resistance to tyranny is obedience to God.' "

Judge Hunt must have had strict orders not only to see that the defendant was convicted, but to do everything he could to prevent the case from going on to a higher court. He allowed Susan to walk out of the courtroom without imposing a prison sentence in lieu of[5] her unpaid fine. If he had sent her to prison, she could have been released on a writ of habeas corpus[6] and would have had the right to appeal. As it was, the case was closed.

▲ ▲ ▲

Although she was disappointed that her case would not go to the Supreme Court as she had originally hoped, Susan knew that she had struck an important blow for woman's suffrage. Henry Selden's arguments and her own speech at the end of the trial were widely publicized, and Judge Hunt's conduct of the trial stood as proof that women were treated unjustly before the law.

Susan did not forget the election inspectors who had allowed her to cast her ballot. The men were fined twenty-five dollars each and sent to jail when they refused to pay. In all, they spent about a week behind bars before Susan, through the influence of friends in Washington, obtained presidential pardons for each of them. In the meantime, her followers,

4 **maxim:** wise saying

5 **in lieu of:** in place of

6 **writ of habeas corpus:** a legal document requesting that a person appear in court

who included some of the best cooks in Rochester, saw to it that the men were supplied with delicious hot meals and home-baked pies.

True to her promise, Susan paid the legal expenses for the three inspectors. With the help of contributions from sympathetic admirers, she paid the costs of her own trial. But she never paid that one-hundred-dollar fine. Susan B. Anthony was a woman of her word as well as a woman of courage.

Suffragettes march in New York City, October 23, 1915

Dumb Criminal Tales

BASED ON TRUE STORIES COMPILED BY DANIEL R. BUTLER, LELAND GREGORY AND ALAN RAY

While in the process of committing crimes, some criminals leave behind clues to their identity or do something so obvious that they are arrested on the spot. Why? Maybe they seek attention or subconsciously want to be caught. But most law enforcement people have another explanation: some people are just stupid.

Making It Easy to Get Caught

Just outside Lawrence, Kansas, police were called to an all-night market that had just been robbed. A male Caucasian had brandished a weapon and demanded money from a store employee. After stuffing the money into his pants pocket, he fled down the street. Units in the area responded quickly to the alarm. Within moments, two officers on patrol had spotted a man running behind some houses in a nearby neighborhood. Certain that they had the right man, they gave chase on foot.

But the suspect wasn't really worried. It was dark, he was a very fast runner, and he knew the neighborhood like the back of his hand. He was sure he would have no trouble eluding the cops.

It didn't take long for the fleet-footed suspect to leave the first pair of officers behind, but he was surprised when more officers quickly joined in the chase. Each time the thief would elude one officer, he would be spotted by another. The crook couldn't understand it; he was using his best moves.

At last there were too many officers on the scene who apparently could see quite well in the dark. Our suspect looked frustrated and surprised when he was finally captured.

But he was even more surprised and frustrated once the police told him how they knew where he was all the time. He really hadn't been hard to follow at all, thanks to advanced technology.

The pursuing officers had just followed the lights. Not the infrared lights used for night vision, but the red lights on the heels of the suspect's high-tech tennis shoes—the ones that blinked on and off every time his feet hit the ground.

A Bad Getaway

[A man in Chicago] liked the finer things in life: fast cars, fine art, and expensive jewelry—stuff he couldn't begin to afford. But while peering through the window of the jewelry store, he reckoned his luck was about to change. This was the heist that would get him out of the hole.

Simple: Smash the window, grab the jewelry, and run. Quickly, he spotted a street manhole cover. He pried out the one-hundred-pound disk, hauled it to the window, and heaved it through. He grabbed all the rings, watches, and diamonds he could carry, then took off running. Turning the corner, he almost bowled over a couple doing some late-night shopping. Panicked, he bolted back into the street, heading for an alley, and then disappeared from sight . . . down the open manhole.

Blundered Attempts

A woman who walked into a Mid-Am Bank in Bowling Green, Ohio, and demanded money from the three tellers inside didn't seem like much of a threat at first. She didn't brandish a gun or threaten anyone with violence. . . .

(There were no customers in the bank, just the tellers and one bank officer.) She was just an average-looking middle-aged woman, with nothing really desperate or criminal about her appearance or demeanor.

But then, suddenly, the stakes went up. The woman repeated her demand for money and brandished a small hand-held device. She claimed it was a radio remote control that at the touch of a button would detonate a car bomb outside, leveling the bank and killing them all. The bank employees glanced nervously at one another. It was not a threat to be taken lightly . . . or so it seemed.

Suddenly, one of the tellers grew surprisingly and defiantly bold. "I'm not giving you anything," she said as she walked out from behind the counter to confront the would-be bank robber. This courageous teller was quickly joined by her two associates, who jumped the woman, wrestled her to the ground, and held her there until the police arrived.

What made the tellers think that the woman wouldn't detonate the bomb?

According to [the police chief], "I think their first clue was when they saw 'Sears' on the end of the garage door opener."

▲ ▲ ▲

One bright spring morning in Lafayette, Louisiana, [a man] had the bright idea of robbing a branch of a local bank. [He] had an even more brilliant idea for a low-cost, low-fat, completely disposable disguise. He would cover his entire head with whipped cream.

A few trial runs indicated his idea would work beautifully. The foamy "mask" sprayed on quickly and was easily wiped off. It completely covered any distinguishing marks, even his hair color. And it tasted wonderful, to boot.

Congratulating himself on his innovative idea, the human hot-fudge sundae walked into the bank and approached the teller. Unfortunately, the employees' response to his delicious disguise was just the opposite of what he wanted. The giggles were discreet at first, but when he said, "Put all your money in the sack," the giggles dissolved into open laughter.

By this time the whipped cream was getting warm and beginning to slide. And the teller had long ago punched the silent alarm. Before you could say "banana split," the police arrived. The rapidly melting bank robber was quickly arrested and refrigerated downtown.

HOW ABOUT REALLY DUMB?

An officer in Savannah developed a bold but simple approach to drug busts. This uniformed patrolman would walk up to a known drug house or party and knock on the door. The occupant would answer the door with almost the same greeting every time. In fact, the similarity of the incidents was astounding. Each person reacted in almost the same manner every time the officer tried this very direct approach to crime busting. It went something like this:

Dumb Criminal opens door. "Uh . . . hello, officer. Is the music too loud? Did someone complain?"

"Nah, I just wanted to buy a bag of dope."

"Huh?"

"Do you have a bag of dope I can buy?"

"Well . . . but you're a cop."

"So? Can't I buy a bag of dope?"

"But . . ."

"Hey, I'm cool, okay?"

"Cool. Wait right here."

A minute later, the dumb (and about-to-be arrested) criminal would be selling the uniformed officer a bag of dope.

The bold officer made so many arrests this way that he was promoted to detective in record time. Almost all of his arrests were pleaded out[1] without a trial because the criminals didn't want to admit in court they had sold drugs to a uniformed cop at their own apartment.

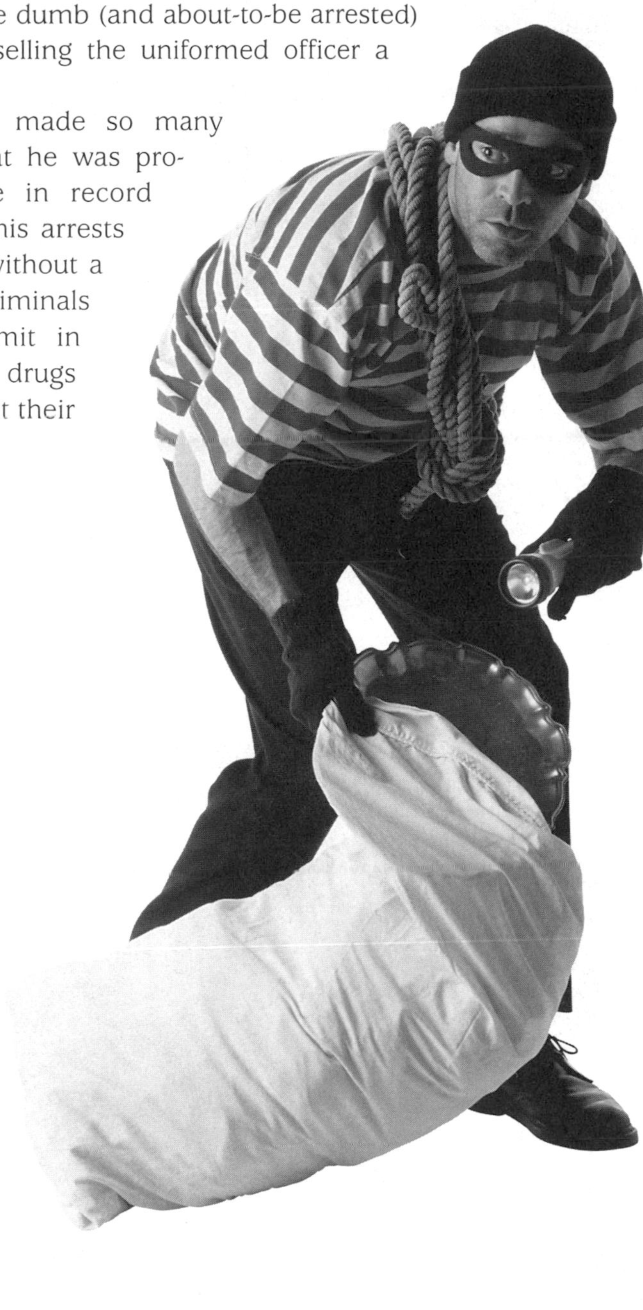

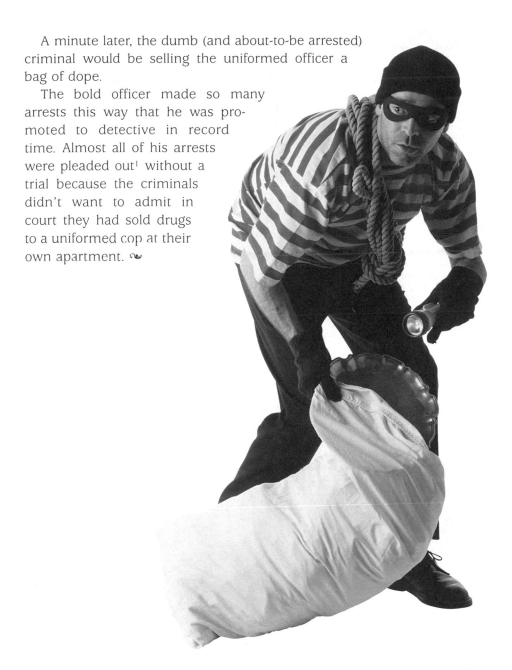

1 **pleaded out:** plea bargained, a negotiation where the defendant is permitted to plead guilty to a reduced charge

The Truth About Sharks

Joan Bauer

The noise seemed faraway at first, like a foghorn blaring in the distance. It was a persistent, ringing, irritating sound. I hated it. I pulled my down comforter over my head, but the noise got louder. It would continue to get louder, too, until I did something. I lifted my head from beneath the covers and saw unhappily that it was morning. I did not do morning, being a devout night person. I gripped the sides of the bed to steady my angst-ridden[1] body and lumbered toward my closet as the noise got louder.

"I hate this!"

I threw open the closet door, lamely stretched my arms upward to find the source of the noise and turn it off, but my mother, the rat, had hidden it well this time. I searched through shoe boxes, purses, then I found it. I grabbed the alarm clock and pushed the on button to off.

Silence.

I dropped to the floor ignoring the knock on my door. All noises were unwelcome in the morning. My smiling mother opened the door and regarded me slumped on the floor.

"There you are."

I shook my head. "It's a mirage."

"Beth," said my mother, "the day has begun; I suggest you do the same. You have to go shopping, wash the dog. . . ."

My mother is a morning person. I made a pitiful noise and curled into a ball.

1 **angst-ridden:** anxious

"Don't push my buttons, Beth. The party starts at five."

I sighed deeply, indicating my level of stress. I didn't see why I had to go to Uncle Al's birthday party that would be nothing but torture because Uncle Al was, basically, subterranean.[2]

"And," my mother ordered, "don't say anything about this party either because Al is my brother who has his faults like all of us do. . . ."

I don't tell sexist jokes at the dinner table.

I don't suck food through my teeth.

"And we're going to go and honor him and make it very clear that we love him."

Nothing came from my lips.

Mother stared at my lips just to make sure nothing would. "You can have the car, Beth, from now until one, then I absolutely have to have it."

"It's ten-thirty already."

"Then you'd better get cracking."

"I hate mornings."

"What a joy you are to me," Mom said and walked off.

I pulled my best black pants from their hanger, the pants I had spent a fortune on, the black pants that now hung dull and lifeless, hopelessly stained by guacamole dip that was dumped on me and them in sheer hostility by Edgar Bromfman when he was doing his Ostrich in Search of a Mate imitation at Darla Larchmont's party. I loved those slacks. They had power.

Once.

They went with my best beaded vest that I wanted to wear to Uncle Al's party because Bianca, my hideous cousin who always dressed to kill, would be there with her latest gorgeous boyfriend to snub me and make me feel insignificant and toady. She learned this from Uncle Al, her father.

Reingold, my black toy poodle, whined torturously at the door. I let him crash in, a rollicking, teeny ball of fur. I picked him up.

"Reingold, you who see all and know all, tell me where in Fairfield County, Connecticut, I can get a vastly important pair of black power pants."

Reingold licked my neck and wiggled.

"Reingold, your wisdom exceeds even your cuteness. Of course, I will go to that new store on Route 1 in Norwalk. And there I will find them."

Reingold followed me into the bathroom. I gave him a drink of water from a little Dixie cup, washed my face fast, brushed my oily brown hair

2 **subterranean:** under the earth's surface

that hung exhausted on my shoulders; I threw on my gray sweats. There was no doubt about it, I looked seedy.

"You're going out like that?" Mom asked, staring.

"Yes." Beauty would come later. All I had going for me now was personality.

Mom touched my bangs. "Maybe if you just—"

I put on sunglasses. "I won't see anyone we know."

▲ ▲ ▲

Mitchell Gail's was a huge store; five stories, to be exact, with too many choices. My mother said that was the problem with the world today—too many choices. Paper or plastic? Regular, premium, or super? Small, medium, or grande?

I walked past the stocky, stern security guard who was picking her teeth, a visual reminder of Uncle Al's bash tonight. Maybe they knew each other. She glared at me through frigid, gray eyes and touched her name tag, MADGE P. GROTON, SECURITY GUARD. The woman needed a life. The sign above her read, SHOPLIFTERS WILL BE PROSECUTED TO THE FULL EXTENT OF THE LAW. I should hope so. I caught sight of myself in a full-length mirror. Who would know that beneath the greasy hair, sallow skin, and baggy sweats there lived a person of depth and significance? I groaned at my vile reflection and headed for the pants section.

I found four pairs of black slacks, size 10, and one pair, size 8. Hope springs eternal. I walked into the dressing room, past another larger, more threatening sign—SHOPLIFTERS WILL BE PROSECUTED TO THE FULL EXTENT OF THE LAW—just in case any thieves missed the first warning. A sweet, round saleswoman showed me to an empty changing room. Her name tag read HANNAH. She had sad eyes.

"If you need anything I'll help you," Hannah said.

"Thanks."

She looked down.

"Must be the pits working on Saturday," I offered.

She shook her head. "I'd rather work. It's better than sitting home. My boyfriend was cheating on me with this manicurist. I saw them kissing in his apartment."

"I'm sorry."

She laughed, not happily. "He said he never really loved me; I was too fat." She looked at her plump arms.

"He's a jerk. You're not fat."

"I'm just going to work, save my money—"

"—Hannah!" It was the store manager. Hannah shrugged stiffly, let out a long, painful breath, and left.

Males. I was between them at the moment. Probably just as well given my last boyfriend's sizzling attraction to blondes—a little problem we were never able to work out since I'm a brunette. I observed a moment of silence for Hannah's pain. Then I tried on the size 8 pants. I could zip them up exactly one-eighth of an inch.

Okay . . . size 8 is still a dream.

On went a size 10.

No.

Another. . . .

Thunder-thighs.

The fourth pair hit me mid-calf.

I tried the fifth. Not bad. I turned in front of the mirror. Not perfect, but doable. And with my beaded vest these could be downright smashing. I put on my shoes, left my coat and sweatpants in the changing room with my purse underneath them. I shouldn't leave my purse there, but I was in such a hurry. I said to Hannah, "I'll take these, but I'm going to keep looking."

"They look nice on you."

They do, don't they? I smiled at the beckoning sale sign over a rack of pants right by the elevator that I'd not seen before. I walked toward the rack and was just reaching for an excellent pair of size 10 black silk pants marked 50 percent off, which would keep me within my budget, which would be a miracle, when a rough hand came down hard on my shoulder and spun me around.

"That's not the way we play the game," Madge P. Groton, Security Guard, barked.

"What?"

"That's not the way we play the game," she repeated, pulling my hands behind my back and pushing me forward.

"What are you talking about?"

She was strong. She pushed me past a line of staring customers, into the elevator. She squeezed my hands hard. A cold fear swept through me.

"What," I shouted, *"are you doing?"*

"You were going into the elevator wearing pants you didn't pay for. We call that shoplifting around here."

"No, I was—"

She pressed my hands tighter.

"You're hurting me!"

"Shut up!"

Tears stung my eyes. My chest was pounding. I had seen a TV show about what to do if you're falsely arrested. You don't fight, you calmly explain your position. There was an explanation. I would give the explanation to this person at the right time and I would go home and never set foot in this store again. If I panicked now . . .

The elevator door opened and the guard shoved me forward past the jewelry counter like a mass murderer, past Mrs. Applegate, Uncle Al's nosy neighbor, who stared at me like she wasn't surprised.

"Ma'am, I'm *innocent,*" I said.

"Yeah, and I'm the Easter Bunny." She opened a door that read SECURITY, and pushed me inside to a dingy beige windowless room with the now-familiar sign: SHOPLIFTERS WILL BE PROSECUTED TO THE FULL EXTENT OF THE LAW.

"Please, Ma'am, Ms. Groton . . ."

My whole body was shaking.

"Take them off," she snarled.

"What?"

"Take the pants off. Now."

I stared at her. "You mean here?"

She put her hand on her gun. This was crazy.

"I get a phone call, right?"

"You are in possession of stolen property."

"Ma'am, I know you're trying to do your job. Just listen to me. I was going to buy these pants. I told this to the saleswoman. I left my coat and my pants and my purse in the changing room. Believe me, this is a big—"

"Take them off." She leaned back in her chair, enjoying her power.

I felt my face shaking like tears were exploding inside. I was sick and terrified. My mind reached for anything.

I remembered that article I'd read about sharks. If you're swimming in the ocean and a shark comes at you to attack, hit him in the nose, the expert said.

I looked at Madge P. Groton, Security Shark.

"No, Ma'am. Not until I get my pants back."

She leaned toward me; her face was tight and mean. "You do what I tell you."

I took a huge breath and looked at her hard.

"No, Ma'am."

Her face darkened. She punched a button on a large black phone, said into the receiver, "I've got one. Send a car."

Nausea hit. I choked down vomit. My heart was beating out of my chest. Madge P. Groton, Security Guard, took her handcuffs off her belt and clinked them on the cracked linoleum floor again and again.

"If we could just talk to that saleswoman," I tried, "I think we could clear this—"

"That's not the way we play the game."

I leaned against the wall and pushed down the screaming voice inside that shouted I was innocent because Madge P. Groton had made up her mind and the Easter Bunny himself couldn't change it. And a car was coming for me with police, probably, which meant jail, probably. I could get thrown into jail with dangerous people and no one was going to listen. I'd never get into veterinary school, never see my dreams fulfilled. My life was over at seventeen.

"I need to make a phone call, Ma'am. I need to call my mother."

"I bet you would."

"The law says I get to make a phone call."

"You can do it at the station."

"Ma'am, my purse and coat and pants are still in the changing room."

Nothing.

I checked my watch: 1:10. My mother was waiting for the car. She wouldn't be getting it soon. I lowered my head and started to cry.

"I've seen you kids," she snarled. "You think you can take anything you want, call your parents, cry some fake tears, and it's over, huh? You think wrong."

"I didn't do it."

I jumped at the harsh knock on the door. A big policeman with leathery skin entered with his hand on his gun. He listened to the security guard's story. I told him she'd made a mistake, but it didn't seem to matter. No one believes prisoners.

"Don't ever set foot in this store again," warned Madge P. Groton.

Don't worry, lady.

The policeman took my arm firmly and we walked out of the store, past Mrs. Applegate, past jewelry, and purses, and leather gloves, and scarves, past the Clinique[3] counter with those white-jacketed technicians, to the waiting police car.

3 **Clinique:** a brand of makeup

"You have the right to remain silent," he said the sickening words to me. "You have the right to an attorney. If you do not have an attorney, one will be appointed for you."

He opened the back door of the squad car, I got in crying.

The door shut like a prison gate.

"It wasn't worth it, Miss," he said, got into the front and drove off with Mrs. Applegate staring after us.

I slumped down deep in the seat and looked at my feet because I was sure everyone I'd ever met in my entire, complex life saw me in the prisoner section of the squad car.

"Officer," I whispered, "I know you're doing your job. I know that security guard was doing hers, but I've got to tell you, if we go back to that store, I've got a witness who knows that I didn't do it."

This was a definite gamble. I didn't know if that saleswoman would remember me.

"Who?" he asked.

I told him about the saleswoman. "Officer, I am really scared and I don't know what else to do. Would you let me try to prove I'm innocent?"

He stopped the car and stared at me through the grill.

"Look, sir, I know I look really weird. I had to buy some slacks for my uncle's stupid birthday party and my mother needed the car in a hurry, so I just jumped out of bed and hadn't figured on getting arrested. I mean, I normally bathe. I normally look better than this. Corpses look better than I do right now. I sound like an idiot."

The policeman searched my face. "Which salesperson?"

I put my two innocent hands on the grill. "Her name was Helen. No. Hortense. Wait—*Hannah*. Yes! She had just broken up with her boyfriend who had been cheating on her for months with this manicurist and he said he'd never really loved her because she was too fat, which she wasn't—a little plump, maybe, but definitely not fat—and she was giving up men. At least for the moment."

He stared at me.

"Not that men are bad. I mean, some are. But you know that. You arrest bad people and that's a really good thing."

I was digging my own grave. He would take me to the psychiatric hospital. I would be locked in a room with no sharp objects. I looked away.

"*Please* believe me, Officer. I'm not really this strange!"

The officer sighed deeply. "I don't have time for this." He rammed the patrol car into gear, did a perfect U-turn, and headed back toward

Mitchell Gail's.

"Oh, thank you, Officer! You are a wonderful person, a—"

He held up his hand for me to stop. I bit my tongue. I didn't ask what would happen if Hannah wasn't there or didn't remember me or was Madge P. Groton's best friend.

▲ ▲ ▲

"Don't try anything funny," said the officer as he opened the squad car prisoner door and I got out.

"I won't." This was the most humorless situation I'd ever been in.

"I do the talking."

I nodded wildly. We walked through the front door, past jewelry, purses, and Madge P. Groton, who nearly dropped her fangs when she saw us.

"Just checking something out," said the officer to her and kept on walking to the elevator.

"What floor were you on?" he asked me.

I held up four trembling fingers.

"You can talk when I talk to you."

"Right," I croaked.

The elevator came and Madge P. Groton glared at us with poison death darts as we got in. I figured an actual policeman was more powerful in the food chain than a security guard, but I decided not to ask at this moment.

The elevator stopped at every floor. A little girl got on with her mother, looked at me and said, "What's the matter with her, Mommy?"

"Polly," said the mother, "don't be rude."

The elevator opened at the fourth floor. We got out. My eyes searched for Hannah. The policeman walked up to a gray-haired saleswoman.

"We're looking for Hortense," he said.

"Hannah!" I shrieked.

The woman pointed to Hannah who was folding sweaters and arranging them on a shelf. We walked toward her. Remember me? I wanted to shout. I am the person who took time from my busy schedule to listen to your problems with your scuzzy boyfriend; the person who cared enough to show you the healing touch of humanity during a particularly stress-packed morning in my life.

"Do you know this young woman?" the policeman asked Hannah.

Hannah looked at me and smiled. "I waited on her this morning. She left her purse and coat and stuff in the changing room. I've got them for you."

Madge P. Groton stormed up. "What's going on?"

"Just clearing a few things up," said the officer.

Madge P. Groton dug in her spurs. "This girl is a shoplifter. I caught her trying to leave the store wearing merchandise!"

Hannah looked shocked. "Then why would she leave her purse in the changing room?"

Why indeed?

I smiled broadly at Madge P. Groton, Security Guard, whose face had turned a delightful funeral gray.

"And why would she leave her coat?" Hannah continued. "It's worth at least as much as the pants. You made a mistake, Madge."

"Can I see the purse?" asked the officer.

Hannah ran to get it. I winced as he pulled out Tums, dental floss, breath mints, two hairbrushes, my giant panda key ring, a box of Milk Duds, three packs of tissues, my sunglasses, four lipsticks.

"You got a wallet in here?"

I reached deep within and pulled it out. He checked my driver's license. He counted the money. Seventy-five dollars.

"I think," said the officer, "we've got things straightened out here, wouldn't you say so, Ms. Groton?"

Madge P. Groton sputtered first. Her wide jaw locked. Her thick neck gripped. Her nose mole twitched. She turned on her scuffed heel and stormed off. The officer gave me back my purse, coat. "You're free to go," he said. "Just give the store back the pants."

"I never want to see these pants again. Thank you for believing me, Officer . . . um . . . I don't know your name."

"Brennerman."

What a wonderful name. I thanked him again.

I thanked Hannah.

I thanked God.

I ran into the changing room, put on my dear, old gray grubbies, drew a penetrating breath of freedom, and raced toward my mother's Taurus. It was two-thirty. All I had to worry about now was the flaming war spear my mother would have singeing[4] the lawn in honor of my late return.

I floored the Taurus, most unwise, since I'd had one brush with the law already today. I drove home, three miles under the speed limit (a first), thanking God I was a free American.

4 **singeing:** scorching

I turned left at the Dunkin' Donuts on Route 1 feeling something wasn't quite right.

I stared at the poster of the cholesterol-laden Dunkin' Munchkins nestled cozily in their box as the unrighteousness of it grew in my soul.

I'd been publicly humiliated.

Falsely accused.

I have my rights!

I rammed Mom's car around and headed back for Mitchell Gail's.

I am teenager, hear me roar.

I parked the car, stormed into the store past the SHOPLIFTERS WILL BE PROSECUTED TO THE FULL EXTENT OF THE LAW sign, right past Madge P. Groton, Security Neanderthal, to the Clinique counter.

"I need to see the store manger," I announced to a blond woman demonstrating face cream. "Immediately."

"Third floor, left by Donna Karan,[5] left by lingerie, you're there."

Madge P. Groton was now guarding the elevator. I took the stairs two at a time, rounded left by Donna Karan, left by lingerie to the store office.

"Can I help you?" asked a tired receptionist with too red hair.

"Only if you're in charge, Ma'am. I need to see the manager."

She looked me up and down. "He's busy now." She looked toward the manager's closed office door. The sign read: THOMAS LUNDGREN, STORE MANAGER.

"It can't wait."

"I'm afraid it's going to have to, dear, you see . . ."

"No, Ma'am. You see. I was falsely arrested in this store by Madge P. Groton, Security Witch, and in exactly two seconds I'm going to call a very large lawyer."

"*Oh, Mr. Lundgren!*" The woman's bony hands fluttered in front of her face. She flew into his office. I walked in behind her. "We have a little problem."

Thomas Lundgren, Store Manager, appraised my grubby gray sweats, unimpressed. "What problem is that?" he said coarsely, not getting up.

I told him. The policeman, Hannah, Madge, the lawyer.

He got up.

"Sit down," he purred at me. "Make yourself comfortable. Would you like a soda? *Candy?*"

5 **Donna Karan:** a fashion designer; in this instance, it means clothes designed by her

"I'd like an apology."

"Well, of course, we at Mitchell Gail's are appalled at anything that could be misconstrued—"

"—This wasn't misconstrued."

"We'll have to check this out, of course."

I folded my arms. "I'll wait, Mr. Lundgren."

"Call me Tom." He snapped his finger at the receptionist. "Get Madge up here."

I crossed my legs. "I'd call the police, too, Tom. Officer Brennerman. He's probably the most important one, next to the lawyer."

Tom grew pale; the receptionist twittered. "Make this happen, Celia," he barked. Then he smiled at me big and wide. "We certainly pride ourselves on treating our customers well."

I smiled back and didn't say he had a long way to go in that department. The phone buzzed and Tom lunged for it. Maybe I'd can veterinary school and become a lawyer. Lawyers have power. No one gets worked up when you say you're going to call a veterinarian.

"I see." Tom said into the receiver. "I see. . . . Yes, Officer Brennerman, it was most unfortunate . . . a vast misunderstanding . . . thank you." He pushed a stick of Wrigley's toward me and mouthed, "Gum?"

I shook my head. Madge P. Groton had seeped into the hall. I said, "By the way, Tom, in addition to false accusations and public humiliation, your security guard told me to take off my pants in her office."

"Pardon?"

"It was a low moment, Tom."

"Tell me you kept them on."

I nodded as Tom moved shakily to the hall, his arms outstretched. "Madge, what is this I'm hearing?"

He shut the office door.

There were hushed, snarling words that I couldn't make out.

I racked my brain to think if I knew any lawyers, large or otherwise. I sort of knew Mr. Heywood down the street, but he was a tax lawyer.

The door opened. Tom grinned. "Madge is truly sorry for the misunderstanding."

Madge glowered at me from the hall. She didn't look sorry.

"Mitchell Gail's is terribly sorry for the . . . inconvenience," he murmured.

"Um, it was a bit more than an inconvenience."

"We would like you to accept a $250 gift certificate from the store for your trouble."

I thought about that.

"We'd be happy to make it $500 for all your trouble," Tom added quickly.

"I'll think about it, Tom."

"We'd really like to get this worked out here and now."

"I'm sure you would, Tom, but I'm going to think about it."

I walked into the hall, past Madge P. Groton, who was so penitent she looked like she'd bitten into a rancid lemon; past Celia, who was fluttering by the receptionist desk. I walked down the stairs and out the door.

Yes!

It was three thirty-seven. All I had to fear now was my mother. I rehearsed my poignant speech all the way home. I was encouraged pulling into the driveway that there was no flaming spear on the lawn. Only a mother spitting fire.

"Mother, you're never going to believe what happened to—"

"You're dead."

I wasn't, of course. Even a profoundly angry parent cannot stay that way long when their beloved child has been falsely accused. It was all I could do to prevent Mom from driving back to the store and personally annihilating Madge P. Groton.

I was the hit of Uncle Al's party. I wore an old black dress, but there was something shining in my face that I could feel—something, Mom said, that money could not buy—empowerment. Mrs. Applegate had called my Aunt Cassie to report on my shoplifting, and even though Aunt Cassie had questioned my innocence, when I told her about Officer Brennerman, she turned pink and flustered and hurried away. I even took Uncle Al aside and told him that the joke he told before dinner offended me and all women through the ages and he *apologized.*

As for my cousin Bianca, she will probably always have a more glamorous life than me, but for a few brief moments that night it really didn't matter.

And regarding Tom and Madge, I decided to not call a lawyer. Tom upped the gift certificate to $650 and had Madge P. Groton personally apologize to me, which was like watching a vulture telling a half-eaten mouse that he didn't really mean it.

"I'm sorry for the trouble," she snarled.

Tom glared at her.

"It was wrong of me," she added flatly.

"Thank you," I said.

Madge P. Groton backed out the door fast and ran down the hall. It was a great moment. Tom said she was going to work in another store and hoped that I would come in often and bring all my friends. I hoped the store was in Antarctica.

I clutched my $650 gift certificate and embraced budget-free shopping. I found the black pants that had started all the trouble—they were marked down 40 percent now—so I got them along with a cherry-apple-red pants suit and a leather jacket and four pairs of shoes and a silk blouse for my mother, who kept saying how proud she was that I had handled this by myself.

I guess I'd learned the truth about sharks: If one comes barrelling at you, the best thing to do is hit it in the nose.

Martin Luther King, Jr.

Gwendolyn Brooks

A man went forth with gifts.

He was a prose poem.
He was a tragic grace.
He was a warm music.

He tried to heal the vivid volcanoes.
His ashes are
        reading the world.

His Dream still wishes to anoint
        the barricades of faith and of control.

His word still burns the center of the sun,
        above the thousands and the
        hundred thousands.

The word was Justice. It was spoken.

So it shall be spoken.
So it shall be done.

RESPONDING TO CLUSTER FOUR

Thinking Skill SYNTHESIZING

1. Each of the other clusters in this book is introduced by a question that is meant to help readers focus their thinking about the selections. What do you think the question for Cluster Four should be?

2. How do you think the selections in this cluster should be taught? Demonstrate your ideas by joining with your classmates to:

   a. create discussion questions

   b. lead discussions about the selections

   c. develop vocabulary activities

   d. prepare a cluster quiz

REFLECTING ON *AND JUSTICE FOR ALL*

Essential Question WHAT IS JUSTICE?

Reflecting on this book as a whole provides an opportunity for independent learning and the application of the critical thinking skill, synthesis. *Synthesizing* means examining all the things you have learned from this book and combining them to form a richer and more meaningful view of justice.

There are many ways to demonstrate what you know about justice. Here are some possibilities. Your teacher may provide others.

1. After reading this book, you should have a better idea of the issues related to justice. Study the issue of capital punishment and prepare and present a debate either in support of or in opposition to the following statement.

   Resolved: Capital punishment is a cruel and unusual form of punishment.

2. Individually or in small groups, develop an independent project that demonstrates what you have learned about justice. For example, you might give a presentation on the problems associated with societal issues of overcrowded prisons, parole reporting, crime rates, etc. Or you may wish to speak to personal justice issues such as family rules. Other options might include a music video, dance, poem, performance, drama, or artistic rendering on a related topic.

Acknowledgments

Text Credits CONTINUED FROM PAGE 2 "Crossing the Line" by Nell Bernstein, from *Seventeen* Magazine, March 1998. Copyright © 1998. Reprinted courtesy of *Seventeen* Magazine and the author.

"Innocent Have I Been Tortured, Innocent Must I Die" from *Witches and Witch-Hunts: A History of Persecution* by Milton Meltzer. Copyright © 1999 by Milton Meltzer. Reprinted by permission of Scholastic, Inc.

"justice" by w. r. rodriguez, appeared in *Welcome to Your Life: Writings from the Heart of Young America* (Milkweed Editions, 1998) and in *The Party Train: A Collection of North American Prose Poetry* (New Rivers Press, 1996). Copyright © 1996 by w. r. rodriguez. Reprinted by permission of the author.

"The Law vs. Justice" from *Bad Habits* by Dave Barry. Copyright © 1983 by Dave Barry. Reprinted by permission of the author.

"Martin Luther King, Jr.," by Gwendolyn Brooks. Reprinted by permission of the author.

"The Quality of Mercy" from *Fair is Fair: World Folktales of Justice* by Sharon Creeden. Copyright © 1994 by Sharon Creeden. Reprinted by permission of August House Publishers, Inc., and Marian Reiner Literary Agency.

"Shrewd Todie and Lyzer the Miser" from *When Shlemiel Went to Warsaw & Other Stories* by Isaac Bashevis Singer, pictures by Margot Zemach. Translation copyright © 1968 by Isaac Bashevis Singer and Elizabeth Shub. Pictures copyright © 1968 by Margot Zemach. Reprinted by permission of Farrar, Straus and Giroux, LLC.

"Someone Who Saw," reprinted with the permission of Atheneum Books for Young Readers, an imprint of Simon & Schuster Children's Publishing Division from *Rearranging and Other Stories* by David Gifaldi. Copyright © 1998 David Gifaldi.

Excerpt from Chapter 2, "This Isn't Kiddy Court; It's Criminal College," from *Don't Pee on My Leg and Tell Me It's Raining* by Judy Sheindlin. Copyright © 1996 by Judy Sheindlin and Josh Getlin. Reprinted by permission of HarperCollins Publishers, Inc.

"The Truth About Sharks" by Joan Bauer, from *From One Experience to Another* edited by M. Jerry and Helen S. Weiss (Tor Books, 1997). Copyright © 1997 by Joan Bauer. Reprinted by permission of St. Martin's Press, LLC.

"The United States v. Susan B. Anthony" from *Women of Courage* by Margaret Truman. Text copyright © 1976 by Margaret Truman. By permission of William Morrow & Company, Inc.

"Words" by Dian Curtis Regan. Copyright © 1998 by Dian Curtis Regan. First appeared in *Dirty Laundry: Stories About Family Secrets*, edited by Lisa Rowe Fraustino, published by Viking. Reprinted by permission of Curtis Brown, Ltd.

Every reasonable effort has been made to properly acknowledge ownership of all material used. Any omissions or mistakes are not intentional and, if brought to the publisher's attention, will be corrected in future editions.

Photo and Art Credits Cover and Title Page: © 2000 Norman Rockwell Family Trust. Photo courtesy of The Norman Rockwell Museum at Stockbridge. Pages 4–5: © Jonathan Blair/CORBIS. Page 8: © Stone Images/Jonathan Morgan. Pages 10–11: (clockwise from bottom left): © Jonathan Blair/CORBIS, © Kevin Schafer/CORBIS, www.arttoday.com, www.arttoday.com, Cyberphoto, www.arttoday.com, © Mike Zens/CORBIS, www.arttoday.com, © Archivo Iconografico, S.A./CORBIS, © Earl & Nazima Kowall/CORBIS, www.arttoday.com; Background: Library of Congress. Page 13: © Joseph Sohm; ChromoSohm Inc./CORBIS. Page 14: © Stone Images/Jean Lannen. Pages 14–15, 23: © Phil Schermeister/CORBIS. Page 17: © Albert Normandin/Masterfile. Page 24: AP/WIDE WORLD PHOTOS. Pages 31: © Stone Images/Mark Gervase. Page 32: David David Gallery, Philadelphia/SuperStock. Page 36 (top to bottom): Everett Collection, Everett Collection, © Picture Quest, © Bettmann/CORBIS. Pages 36–37: © Stone Images/Hunter Freeman. Page 39: © Picture Quest. Page 41: (foreground) © Collection of Fall River Historical Society (background) The Standard-Times. Page 51: © Stone Images/Colin Hawkins. Pages 52–53: © Tim Flach/CORBIS. Pages 52, 55: © Mindy Myers. Page 56: #70 "A Porter at rest. Warsaw, 1937." From *A Vanished World* by Roman Vishniac. Copyright © 1983 by Roman Vishniac. Reprinted by permission of Farrar, Straus & Giroux, Inc. Page 61: © Victor Brel/Image Concept. Pages 62–63: © Stone Images/Rod Long. Page 64: © Stone Images/Laurence Monneret. Page 71: © The Purcell Team/CORBIS. Page 77: © 1999 Doug Hopfer. Page 81: © Stone Images/Natalie Fobes. Page 82: © Eugène Delacroix/Picture Quest. Page 87: Ellen Terry (1847–1928) as Portia (litho) by Louise Jopling (1843–1933) (after) Private Collection/The Stapleton Collection/Bridgeman Art Library. Page 88: Musée des Beaux-Arts, Tournai. Page 99: Amsterdam, Van Gogh Museum (Vincent Van Gogh Foundation). Page 102: Everett Collection. Page 111: © Michael Carroll/SIS. Pages 112–113, 122: Library of Congress. Page 125: © Stone Images/Christopher Bissell. Page 127: Digital imagery® copyright 1999 PhotoDisc, Inc. Page 128: © Stone Images/Steven Rothfeld. Page 142: © Bettmann/CORBIS.